T0167206

The Journey of an Aging Professor

With Some Theological Reflections
along the Way

William J. Rademacher

Order this book online at www.trafford.com
or email orders@trafford.com

Most Trafford titles are also available at major online book retailers.

Printed in the United States of America.

ISBN: 978-1-4269-8850-9 (sc)
ISBN: 978-1-4269-8851-6 (e)

Trafford rev. 09/15/2011

www.trafford.com

North America & international
toll-free: 1 888 232 4444 (USA & Canada)
phone: 250 383 6864 • fax: 812 355 4082

Foreword

Foreword by Dr. David McNamara

Revelation is much more than the final book of New Testament Scripture. It is an ongoing journey – a true *adventure* – to which each of us is invited. And while some prefer to pass along life's path taking little heed of the revelatory messages sent their way by a loving Creator, those better informed among us tend to savor each rich moment of discovery. Whether painful or blissful, the value of revelation resides in our response to it and in our ability to grow from every experience – ideally leading us toward a closer relationship with God and with our fellow human beings.

This idea has been underscored time and time again in my own journeys, traversing most countries in the Western Hemisphere. Circumstances and messengers of revelation have varied wildly, but my own humanity has provided the constant interpretive lens through which, each time, I have received and processed the message.

From the idiosyncratic symphony orchestra musicians with whom I have worked to the humblest of mountain folk in remote Mexican and Guatemalan villages, I have learned. And in more recent years working in diocesan ministry settings, clergy and lay people alike have taught me well. But the journey has not ended and the learning continues.

Dr. Rademacher's book, *The Journey of an Aging Professor*, offers readers an insight into the author's experiences on the path of life. From humble beginnings in rural Michigan, through seminary and priestly life, to the contemporary analytical maturity of a retired professor, Dr. Rademacher shares wisdom garnered from careful contemplation of his life's many revelatory adventures.

Not a stranger to controversy, Dr. Rademacher regularly challenges his readers to broaden their understanding of the Church, its traditions, and its teachings. From the role of *all* lay persons in Church precincts to today's growing multi-cultural face of Roman Catholicism in the United States, the writer paints a picture of an ecclesial landscape begging for inclusivity.

This author's analysis of milestones traversed during his life's journey presents us, the People of God, with a clear challenge to preserve and expand the same dynamism that has sustained and nurtured our Church for two millennia. Indeed, if we are to prosper in the future as a living "Body of Christ," Dr. Rademacher's thoughts – and innate qualities – are most worthy of our consideration and potential emulation.

My hope is that, like Dr. Rademacher, each of us might heed our Creator's daily revelations to us as we persevere in our own journey toward God.

June 30, 2011

J. David McNamara, D.Min.

Director of Education and Formation / Roman Catholic Diocese of Las Cruces

Contents

The Journey of an Aging Professor

Endorsements for the Back Cover

I Dr. Rademacher invites us to accompany him as he journeys from the farm of his boyhood to the universities where he has taught. His itinerary reveals his own maturing and reflects the evolving of the Church he loves and has served so well.

Donald A. Dohr

Introduction

Why a Memoir

By William J. Rademacher Ph.D.

Maybe the world will be enriched by my unique story? Or, maybe the world will be bored to death? Maybe there's no one out there who gives a hoot? When my pall bearers come, the stampede to Walmart will continue. Life, such as it is, will go on, memoir or no memoir.

So a memoir is one continuation of the life of that saving Word. It is a new dawn in the midst of the darkness. Parts of the world may pause to admire this dawn which is indeed new every day. As such, my memoir can be a treasure for those who want to see a new dimension of that Word, ever revealing new sparks of infinity. My poor written words go beyond themselves when they take flesh in my fellow pilgrims. A life with many flaws is still healed by the Word's many miracles. While the blood-stained cross has been part of my journey, there have been many more Easter alleluias. And it's always these Easter alleluias that light up my day until the sun knows no setting.

Before going any further, it's time to recall the two major rules for writing a memoir. First, I have to be honest. Being honest is more than just telling the truth. It means trying to be complete and include those parts I would rather omit. This includes my painful relation to my father and my joy and struggle of falling in love. And this leads me into the second rule: to banish the scourge of self-consciousness. This will be tough for an introvert like myself. Even now my counselor is trying hard to get me to be more assertive. It is indeed one way to overcome depression. To my amazement writing a memoir is good medicine for my tendency to escape into a closet of introverts. To have a normal social life one just has to be engaged in all the dynamics of life in the public sphere. The lonely life on the farm and the life of silence in the seminary were powerful factors in building a permanent search for a monastic retreat. But, with the help of my counselor I am determined to move into a more assertive engagement with the world about me. Writing an honest memoir requires uncovering the precious secrets of life. After a memoir those secrets will be secrets no longer. It's no wonder that St. Augustine called his memoir "Confessions." It's a good word to describe all those secrets that are a living part of life's journey. So, onward we go. Sometimes the struggle continues.

So why should anyone pause to read my words, the poor symbols which try to mirror the awesome mystery of one life on this spinning planet? Are the words just words meant to feed the author's ego? Mere words can't possibly convey all the feelings, the tears, the blood, the sweat, the joys or the ecstasy of one human journey. The selective memory of an old man will recall only bits and pieces etched in the brain moving through the years. But yet, amazingly, these pieces still carry hints of the broader mystery of life. As such, they have their own value. They are precious. They are so many windows open to the Creator Who walks with all of us humans from sunrise to sundown, from cradle to grave.

Even so, my journey has been hard. Often I pray with Francis Thompson: "Ah! Must Thou char the wood ere Thou canst limn with it?" In the dark valley of despair it's easy to feel abandoned by the Lord; easy to feel: "Alack, thou knowest not how little worthy of any love thou art! Whom wilt thou find to love ignoble thee Save Me, save only Me!...Rise, clasp My hand and come!"[1] These last words are the bright rays of an unending dawn. A trumpet blast from the sky!

They help me continue my journey in faith and hope, all the while, clinging fast to His hand.

The Psalmist said it long ago:

O Lord, you have probed me and you know me
You know when I sit and when I stand;
you understand my thoughts from afar.
My journeys and my rest you scrutinize,
with all my ways you are familiar.
Even before a word is on my tongue,
behold, O Lord, you know the whole of it.
Behind me and before, you hem me in
And rest your hand upon me.
Such knowledge is too wonderful for me;
Too lofty for me to attain.
Truly you have formed my inmost being;
you knit me in my mother's womb.
I give you thanks that I am
fearfully, wonderfully made.
Your eyes have seen my actions;

---

1 Francis Thompson, *Hound of Heaven*. The Standard Book of British and American Verse. Selected by Nella Braddy, (New York: Garden City Publishing Co.1932), 661.

in your book they are all written.
My days were limited before
one of them existed.
How weighty are your designs
 Oh God!
how vast the sum of them;
If I were to recount them, they
would outnumber the sands;
did I reach the end of them,
I should still be with you. (Psalm 139)

So, clasp my hand. We embark on this journey together. Sometimes we lurch. Some times we fly. But onward we go. Our calendars never go backwards! And every dawn is truly a new gift. This planet abounds with created wonder and God's mysterious presence. At times we are smitten with awe and fall on our knees before the mystery of life. I rejoice that at my age I can still share at least a part of that mystery with my fellow pilgrims.

CHAPTER 1
On the Farm

It's a great blessing to be born on a farm. You grow up in the middle of cute little lambs; cows trudging homeward single file with another day's milk; chickens and roosters who never cease their cackling. In a word, you are surrounded by an amazing variety of life. From the cats and dogs playing with you on the house steps to the horses galloping into the woods, there is never a dull moment. You live in the midst of God's holy creation in the process of becoming.

I remember the verse: "feed my lambs; feed my sheep" (Jn. 21:15;19). It has always intrigued me that Jesus would call the lambs, *my* lambs. Evidently the animals God created in the beginning still belong to Him. Surely the variety of animal life is a powerful symbol of the Creator's own marvelous creativity. On the farm it's much easier to understand that not "one sparrow falls to the ground without the Father's will" (Mt.10:29). An infinite God would surely want to be present in His created world in an infinite number of ways. Surely, that includes the humble sparrows and all the rest of us. God is present not only in Church or in His high heavens, but especially in the life around us.

On our farm we were never far away from the Stony Creek. In the winter it provided a rendevous for ice skating with friends and neighbors. Our clip-on skates were not always reliable. Jumping across sleds, the skates could come off, leaving us sprawling on the ice. It was a wonderful Christmas when Santa Claus brought us shoe skates. Ice skating became a totally new adventure. We hardly ever missed a Sunday afternoon with friends a mile west on our Stony Creek.

In the summer our Stony Creek served as a swimming pool after a hard, sweaty day in the field. We tried our hand at fishing with long sticks and kite strings. But the fish were too small. It just wasn't practical to shave the scales and eat the little creatures. We did make a little pocket money for ourselves by setting traps along the Stony Creek for minks and muskrats. The minks were clever and hard to catch. Often they would turn over the traps and eat the chicken bait. But mink fur brought a good price. So catching a mink was worth the extra effort and a time for extra celebration.

In the spring the Stony Creek would sometimes spill over its banks and our neighbors would lose some of their wheat. Every day the waters would come closer and closer to our house. But thanks be to my mother's nervous prayers, the waters never reached our house. And it was quite a relief for our whole family to watch the waters subside. But the waters spilling over their banks left a fear of floods imbedded in my psyche until this day.

It was a moment of great joy, in more tranquil time, when I could lie down on the grass on the banks of Stony Creek and listen to the birds singing to each other. We had a few wild canaries, but it was the simple sparrows who did most of the singing. They were always in great abundance. It's a homely bird to be sure, but always ready to sing for us who were willing to listen.

In Michigan we had four distinct seasons. And we were never in doubt about what season it was: fierce cold in winter and sweaty heat in summer. Our lives just had to be in rhythm with the changing seasons. Most of our planting of corn, beans, oats and barley occurred in the spring. Only the wheat was planted in the fall. The hardest work came with all the harvests in the fall. Putting heavy bundles of corn in upright "shocks" was not child's work. But we did it as children.

Two horses hitched to a "bean puller" pulled the beans. Pitch forks in hand, we put the beans in small mounds to dry. Later we hauled all the beans into the barn. The bean thresher would come in late fall. Beans were mostly a cash crop, but often they did end up on our dinner table in delicious soups.

Our struggle with the weeds began at an early age. I'm sure I was not older than six when I had to tackle weeds almost my size with a sharp, curved blade and handle. But the weeds were nothing compared to the large "bull thistles." These required several strokes from a relative distance. Even the plow horses kept their distance from these thistles, veering sharply to the right or left as I tried, at a later age, to control the plow.

It was wonderful to see a field full of ripe wheat, waves flowing gently with the wind. But a storm of wind and rain could level the field in a matter of hours. That meant the whole field of wheat was lost. So, it was a moment of great joy when, in mid summer, our horses pulled the binder into the field. Harvesting wheat meant cutting the wheat and then standing up the bundles in shocks to dry. A few days later it was time to pitch the bundles on the wagon and haul them all to the barn where they would wait for the threshing machine. On threshing day all the neighbors, it seemed, came to help. And at the end of the day there was always a big dinner for all of us hungry threshers.

Fall, as noted, was the time for more harvests. We relied heavily on corn because it was the staple food for both cows and pigs. There was only one advantage: we could stay home from school on the day the harvester cut the corn. But there were times when most of our family of eight preferred school to the heavy drudgery in the field. In those days most everything was done by hand. But it was a happy time. A full harvest could hardly be otherwise since it represented the fruit of the summer's struggles with the weeds. A full harvest was truly a family victory! Tired, but happy, we washed up for a delicious chicken dinner at the end of the day.

On our farm we also grew sugar beets and peppermint. After our summer struggle with the weeds we had to cut the peppermint by hand cutters. Our cousins had a truck large enough to haul the peppermint to another cousin's farm for distillation. When the big tanks were full and well packed down, our cousins would introduce the steam which went through the whole tank and separated the leaves from the precious peppermint oil. Peppermint oil left a powerful but delightful odor on our clothes. It was a unique and complicated process to extract the peppermint oil. But, like the sugar beets, it brought in much needed cash.

The hardest part with the sugar beets was the topping process: cutting the leaves from the "tops" of each beet. We stacked the beets and covered them with their leaves so they would not dry out while waiting for the truck to arrive to take them to the processor. Beets were heavy and at least once the weight produced a blowout on our cousin's truck. We bought our own sugar in 100 lb. bags at the processing plant. We stored them upstairs for family use. Even during the rationing of World War II we were never out of sugar in our house.

The farm was always a whole family project. There were eight of us. I had two sisters older than myself and two sisters younger. And often my four sisters were out in the fields with us from sun-up to sun-down.

During the war, when my older brother was drafted into the army, my sister, Marie, pitched the bundles up to me to load on the wagon. Whether it was milking the cows or driving the horses, there never was any gender distinction. Four women could do whatever the boys could do. The only exception was lifting the 80 lb. bags of fertilizer. That was a "man's job."

But home life was difficult, not only because of our poverty but also because of the harsh discipline imposed by my father. There never were any words of encouragement for any of the completed tasks. And there were many scoldings for my minor failures in the work on the farm. And I will never forget his repeated prediction: "You will never amount to anything." I know now he said this because he suspected I would never be a farmer. And for him that meant "amount to nothing." Otherwise, our family life was probably as normal as most families.

Like most families we never got any sex instructions. Sex was simply never mentioned by anybody in our family. Silence seemed to be the unwritten and unspoken law. But I never considered it a great loss. After all, the cows and the pigs, doing what comes naturally, gave us a visual instructions on sex almost daily. It was not hard to figure out that human babies were produced just like animal babies. Of course, the animals did not teach us any moral responsibility relating to sex. So, unfortunately, sex remained at the animal level. We had to apply our own catechism instructions to lift sex to God's holy creation. But mostly the catechism said: "It's a big sin; don't do it."

It was a happy day when my father bought a Ford tractor. The era of horses was over. Soon, at age fifteen, I found myself plowing the field with our new tractor. It was a welcome relief from the days of trudging behind two horses and a plow. Life on the farm would never be the same. We used the tractor in hundreds of ways. It meant that most of our horse tools had to be converted so they could be pulled by a tractor. We were part of a new era in the history of farming. Our tractor was small, but it was a symbol of the revolution taking place in the so called "simple" life of the farm.

As strict Catholics we always prayed before and after meals and prayed the Rosary together every evening before going to bed. With great sacrifice our parents sent us to St. Mary's Catholic School five miles away. The Sisters were strict teachers. So we did learn our Catholic Faith rather well. But we also made friends. It was a welcome change from the loneliness on the farm. We had to walk five miles on the way home when weather permitted. And that was quite a chore with books for homework and a lunch bucket. Sometimes our neighbors would pick us up. That was moment of great joy.

With a family of eight there was rarely a dull moment at the supper table. With four boys and four girls we had a happy mix. We shared the events of the day whether good or bad. As we grew older, boy friends and girl friends became part of the conversation. There was very little that was strictly private. As long as we used no cuss words, we all felt quite free to participate in the dinner conversation.

But breakfast was the time when my father might issue the orders for the day. It was an extremely painful moment one day when he told us that we had to shoot our pet dog "because he is blind and running into fences. It is cruelty to animals to let them suffer that way." So after finishing the morning chores, my older brother and I took "Brownie" into the woods. My older brother had his 18 gauge shot gun on his shoulder. We were both too sad to say anything as we walked our dear pet into the woods.

Once in the woods my brother shot Brownie with one shot. We walked back home in silence with lumps in our throats. It was a sad day indeed. Until the tears came, I did not realize how attached I had become to our Brownie. When it comes to the emotions I can fake it only so long.

Emotions are real. They are a living part of my humanity. I just can't live in the abstract. The emotions won't let me, no matter how hard I try to repress them.

I will never forget our wonderful orchard full of a variety of apple trees. When the apples were ripe we picked up a bunch of our favorite cider apples and took them along into the field. We also stored bushels of apples in our basement to take to school and to eat during the winter months. Then came the day when we filled our trailer with cider apples and took them to town to fill three or four barrels with cider. My father liked the cider. Most of us children enjoyed the cider, too, on the hot days when we were bringing in the hay.

I will never forget the day when we had to go to the woods and cut down all the trees my Father had marked. With saw and axe on our shoulders, my brother and I went into the woods and discovered twenty-five trees had been marked for cutting. It was tricky to throw the trees in the right direction. But it was a challenge we enjoyed. Once the trees were on the ground we had to cut them into logs short enough to pull them home with our team of horses and a log chain.

After World War II came to end, my older brother came home from the army. Life went back to normal. My sister, Marie, no longer had to help me milk the cows and do the chores at night. It was a day of great joy for my father. He was a staunch Republican and came close to tears when my brother was drafted to fight in "Roosevelt's war," as he called it.

The only good thing Roosevelt did, according to my father, was to bring electricity to the farmers in 1938. It was called the REA, the Rural Electric Administration.. From then on, we no longer had to milk the cows with a flickering lantern. It was always difficult to do the chores in the semi-darkness of one lantern. Electricity was the beginning of a new era on our farm.

One of the first big jobs my brother and I had to tackle was painting the barn. I was still quite young and it seemed like an impossible job for the two of us to paint our big barn. But my brother said: “Why don’t you paint this door? I will paint the higher levels.” After I finished the first door, I was assigned a second door. And so it went, one door at a time. It taught me an important lesson: no matter how impossible the task appears at first sight, we can always tackle the job one door at a time. It was a time of great joy when we finally finished painting the whole barn.

We did not celebrate for long. Within days we had to start on the house. That required more care because we had to trim the house with dark green. The windows and the doors were a special challenge. Mother was especially nervous when my brother or I climbed up to the top of the ladder. We did all our painting with a wide brush and a one gallon can. But after all the painting, I was sure I was never going to become a painter.

On my sixth birthday I milked my first cow. From then on I had to milk two cows every morning before I went to school and every evening. Again, all our milking was done by hand with the flickering light of the lantern. Fortunately, my older brother always milked the “kickers.” I always got to milk the gentle cows. When my brother was drafted in the army, I had to milk the “kickers” and my sister, Marie, got to milk the gentle ones.

The lambing season began in the spring. There were always two or three sheep who rejected their own lambs. This was a big mystery. But this meant that my brother and I would get pet lambs that we had to feed every morning and night with a bottle of cow milk. The actual feeding was fun. But the day would come when my father would back the trailer up to the orchard gate and he would take our pet lambs to market. We watched in tears as the car and trailer hit the road. We were more attached to our pet lambs than we realized.

Our little flock of geese never caused any problems. It was fun to watch "mother goose" sit on four or five large eggs for a long time. (The eggs were three times the size of chicken eggs.)

We knew that soon little geese would be born. "Mother goose" stayed in her own old cider barrel for about four weeks. Then suddenly there would appear the cutest little yellow geese you ever saw.

The geese normally were well behaved in the orchard. But one day they surprised us all by taking flight toward the Stony Creek, a half a mile away. My father, with a tone of anger, said: "the geese don't have any water." It was my job to keep the water trough full. And sure enough, the trough was dry. But to everyone's amazement the geese, after drinking water at the creek, came flying back to the orchard. That's where they had corn and other food. While we were used to the high-flying wild geese going south before winter, we never knew our own tame geese could fly that distance to the creek.

We always sold the spring crop of geese just before Thanksgiving. Since many people ate a goose rather than a turkey, the price was always best just before Thanksgiving. Only once did we butcher a goose ourselves. My mother insisted geese were too fat and oily for eating. But most of the family liked the goose. It was a pleasant departure from the usual chicken dinner.

With my father in control neither we nor our horses ever worked on Sunday. Our family often spent Sunday afternoon playing euchre and eating the popcorn my father popped on our old wood-burning stove. It was a bit of family fun since no one ever played for money. But all of us were addicted to the popcorn which we grew in our own garden with every kind of vegetable you can imagine. We all had to take turns hoeing in the garden, although Pa did most of it. We took for granted our table vegetables would be fresh out of the garden. Even as a child, I had to hold out my arms while my father picked the corn at 5:00 p.m.. Then we sat on the porch steps to strip the husks. Mother would take the corn and put them in the boiling pot. It was a wonderful time when our sweet corn was in season. We always had plenty.

Winter was a time to butcher five or six pigs. With a family of eight we needed a lot of pork to get through the winter. We always had help from the neighbors to get through this ordeal. The two hundred pounders we would just catch by hand and my father would stick them in the throat with a butcher knife while my brother held them. It was my job to catch the blood as it flowed from the pig's throat. Then I had to run to the house with the blood, stirring all the while, because of the cold. My mother was always waiting for the blood. We made a lot of blood sausage along with the usual German brats. We had large crocks in the basement to store the butchered pork covered with fat. We had no electricity until 1938 so we had no freezer to store food of any kind.

I must say I enjoyed school most of the time. Most of our sisters were good teachers and we loved most of the subjects. I enjoyed our spelling classes. Sister would have Spelling Bee contests. That meant we would stand up against the wall and take our turn spelling whatever words sister announced. But the best part came when the whole school took the Clinton County spelling test. My older brother and sister had won the Spelling award and we all saw their names in the weekly *Clinton County Republican News.* So the pressure was on me to win that County award. And fortunately, I won the award three years in a row.

I quickly learned that some subjects come easier than others. I always had to struggle with math. I was simply aghast when, during dinner, I would see my father multiply rather large figures in his head. All this happened before the invention of the calculator. But I managed to get good grades in all the other subjects. My father did not get upset at my low marks in math because, as he said, we rarely used that on the farm.

Our farm was two miles from the nearest highway. So, it was always peaceful on the farm. It was only when we walked home from school that we encountered the big noisy trucks. Maybe I was born with a monastic streak, but later in life I often found myself heading to the library just to enjoy the peace and quiet. To this day a walk along the river is wonderful recreation. I get some of my best ideas for writing my weekly column in the *Agua Viva,* our diocesan newspaper, while walking along the river. I enjoyed some of my best moments in my life while canoeing on the river. It's a wonderful place to pursue your contemplative instincts. Or, to write a poem or an article in "your head." And you never know what wonderful new scenery will show up around that next bend in the river.

In my travels I have seen a good part of this spinning earth. But I feel our farm in Michigan is still the best place on earth. The shadows grow longer now. And there may not be many sunsets left. But if I had to do it over again, I would choose to be born on the farm where the birds are singing and multi-colored leaves blowing across the road.

CHAPTER 2
Off to the Seminary

No matter how hard I try, I can't remember a specific day when I felt a call to the priesthood. It was mostly a gradual process. In fact, it was so gradual that I decided to go first to the local high school to have a "year to think it over." But at the end of that year I was fairly sure that God was calling me to the priesthood.

Nevertheless, my vocation was something of a mystery. In the beginning of my time in the seminary, I was not sure I was in the right place and destined to be there for another eleven years. At age fourteen, I wonder if anyone can be sure about a life's vocation. The decision, at least in my case, was more instinct than certitude. I remember well that I liked to read and study. And I knew I was beginning a long period of study. I just knew in my heart that I would like a life of study. I was always attracted to the immense possibilities of learning something new, whatever that might be.

Upon arrival in the seminary I was placed in a special class with other outside high school students who were in a catch-up mode because of their lack of proficiency in Latin. We had to concentrate on Latin for a whole year before we could take our places in the regular second year class. I remember that I was quite sad to discover how difficult it was to master Latin. My grades in Latin were so low I considered quitting the seminary. I was just not prepared for such a struggle. I had received two D's in Algebra in my freshman year in high school. But I hated Algebra and did fine in all the other subjects.

Life in the seminary is hard to describe. In one sense, it is a painful emotional experience to be away from home at such a young age. "Homesickness" is a mild and totally inadequate word to describe the overall experience. Being away from home, from classmates and from the farm was like being in exile. It was not easy for a shy farm boy to make new friends in the seminary.

On the other hand, I was glad to get away from my father's constant scoldings. It was plain that I received more scolding than any of my brothers and sisters. This was a great mystery to me until after my father's death. One evening while I was alone staying with my mother, she shared with me the main reason why my father's scolding was directed more at me than anyone else. Her words were painful to hear even though they were no surprise. From my mother's own lips came the words: "Pa never liked you." Even though I had long suspected that, it was still painful to hear my suspicions confirmed.

Because of my father's severe scoldings, I had often thought about running away from home. But I rejected the idea because it would hurt my mother deeply. I had the feeling that she loved me all the more to make up for my father's scoldings. No doubt going to the seminary was one way of running away from home and those endless scoldings. Even though I did not know what I was running to, I was sure of what I was running from. My motivation was mixed from the beginning. For whatever reason, this did not bother me. I was content with the feeling that most of the time our feelings and our reasons are mixed.

As a strict Catholic I knew I was bound to forgive my father, however painful that might be. And I did manage to forgive him in my heart, although I never mustered the courage to tell him before he died. I was quite aware that Christians are called to forgive and keep forgiving. But forgiving him did not remove the scoldings from my memory. These, no doubt, will go with me to the grave. But the act of forgiving, on the level of feeling, does remove part of the burden from the memory.

There really is no mystery about seminary life. The curriculum of studies is similar to other high schools, except there is considerable emphasis on Latin and Greek. The hardest adjustment is the highly controlled daily life style. No one is allowed to leave the seminary grounds without permission. The average day is fairly well packed with classes and study periods with an hour and a half break in the afternoon for recreation outside. The challenge was to adjust to such tight control, especially when, at that early age, the reasons were not evident

Special Latin was my hardest class for the first year. My grades were so low I continued to think about quitting. But somehow, after much prayer, I kept plugging along. I managed to earn a passing grade and so was permitted to enter the regular second year class beginning with the second semester. Then it was Greek that became the hardest class. Languages were not my strong point. Geometry was more fun. It was a pleasant relief from Algebra which seemed to be the most useless subject ever invented. My father, who knew nothing about Algebra, was quite upset when he saw my two D's on my report card in High School. To please him, I managed to eke out a "C" the next semester.

The years went on with a full load of classes. With my height, I did manage to get on a basketball team. And this was a tremendous relief from the rigor of the classroom schedule.

Sports were the only official escape from the seminary routine. I never got involved with football since I never liked the physical bashing which was the heart of the game. Public Speaking was a rather challenging class. On the farm I grew up in the middle of eight children. It was expected that I remain silent. So I grew up as a shy, timid personality. So Public Speaking was a welcome challenge. I had a good voice and was able to project it effectively. So I got all A's in Public Speaking. This was some consolation in view of a vocation to preach the Gospel on Sundays.

In the final years of the minor seminary the courses became a lot easier. I was able to earn good grades in most of the required subjects. So it was with great joy that in 1948 I graduated from the minor seminary with a *Magna Cum Laude.* It was quite an achievement after the difficult early years. Even some professors were amazed at my progress in five years. But I was happy to leave the minor seminary and its twenty-four hour control of my life. It was a welcome relief to begin the two year course in philosophy at Mt. St. Mary of the West in Cincinnati, Ohio.

From the very beginning I fell in love with philosophy. Scholastic philosophy made a lot of sense to me. The various divisions into Logic, Metaphysics and the history of philosophy were intriguing from beginning to end. I threw myself into these subjects and they absorbed my every minute. I could have continued studying philosophy but it came to an end in two short years. Now it was time to begin Theology, the subject which was more directly connected with the priesthood. I also loved it from the beginning. It was a love which would never end. Eventually it would propel me to pursue the doctorate in theology.

To begin the study of theology I had to go to the new major seminary in Plymouth, Mich. The complete program included four years of theology. By now I was used to being away from home and really did not mind the rigid seminary routine. On leaving home I could not help but remember my father's scoldings. But forgiveness helped me to leave a painful burden behind and to really live the Christian message of unconditional love of neighbor, living or dead. Such unconditional love included continuing forgiveness.

Living in isolation from the world was not difficult for me since living on the farm was already a form of isolation. The course of studies seemed easier than the two years of philosophy. But once again we were confined to the seminary grounds. I did not question the system and lived comfortably within it.

The main text books were all in Latin. But this was no problem since I had finally mastered Latin. It was strange that the same Latin text books were reprinted without change year after year. This produced a static, unchangeable theology. From the beginning this was hard to accept. So I went to the Library to find other books on theology with other opinions. One day in class I made the mistake of quoting a Library text which contradicted the required text book. I remember I found the text quite a refreshing departure from the canned theology we had to memorize for class. But the professor glared at me and in no uncertain terms told me to stick to the required text. I was quite embarrassed to receive such a scolding in front of all my classmates. But I remained convinced there had to be more to theology than a memorization of one Latin text. However, never again did I question a professor or his required text in any class of seminary theology. But I knew in my heart that there was much more to theology than the unchangeable formulas which were supposed to be the answer to every moral question on earth.

In the major seminary I received both the minor and the major orders leading to the priesthood. The minor orders were porter, acolyte, exorcist, and lector; the major orders were subdeacon, deacon and priest. The major orders are not conferred until the last years of theology. Since there were seven orders, the sacrament of Holy Orders is always in the plural.

The order of subdeacon creates considerable anxiety and hard reflection because it is for life. It is a clear movement toward the priesthood since it forbids marriage and requires a vow of chastity for life. It is actually the application of the law of celibacy which applies to all priests of the Latin Rite. The law prompts a lot of reflection on sex and the single life. In the all male culture of the seminary it is hard to reflect realistically about what kind of challenge celibacy will be in the actual life of the priesthood. But eventually, after much prayer and discernment, I decided to go ahead and accept a law which had some obvious benefits in making more time available for ministering to the people in the parish. With long and difficult reflection these practical benefits helped me take a more positive view of the law.

Strangely, I do not remember any spiritual, psychological or theological explanation of the vow of chastity. It was just a non-negotiable condition for entering the priesthood. It seemed so tightly bound to the priesthood that it seemed like a divine law demanded by Jesus Christ, Himself. Of course, we knew from our study of Church History that the law came into being for the Latin Rite only during the Council of the Lateran in 1059. We also knew it was a changeable Church discipline rather than a fixed dogma of the Church. But the problematic psychological implications were never discussed publicly. Adjustment to a single life and the repression of the sexual component of one's humanity was simply a given. Silence was the only permitted response. No one publicly raised any objections to the problems created by the required denial of one's full humanity.

No one taught us that growth to full personhood included healthy relationships with both genders. The psychology and theology of living the rest of our lives under the human law of celibacy was never included in any preparation for the subdeaconate. In retrospect, one could make a rather strong case for the celibate life linked to the priesthood. But no one in an official position made an effort to establish a rationale for the law in terms of improving the quality of priestly service in daily parish life.

This kind of rationale would have to be rooted in basic Christian anthropology. It teaches us that "we are whole and entire only in our relationships with others: both human others and with God, that divine other...to be human means to be-in-relation, to be-with...Christian theology has tended to ignore this, treating human "nature" independently of its sexual concretization."[2]

So ministry, to be really Christian, first and foremost needs to be a living example of what it means to be fully human. Anything less betrays the wholeness of God's holy creation and the incarnation of the human in Jesus Christ, including both genders. For this reason celibacy needs to be understood as an exception to human nature as created and redeemed. Its rationale begins by first asserting that which is fully human. Only then will its meaning as an exception be fully understood.

In 1059 the church and its clerical culture were still not free from the pathology of patriarchy and mysogyny which helped to produce the celibacy law. It's true that clerical simony, lay investiture and the dominance

---

2 John R. Sachs, *The Christian Vision of Humanity*, (Collegeville, MN: The Liturgical Press, 1991), 19.

of the monastic mentality contributed to the acceptance of a law which was part of a much needed reform launched by Pope Gregory VII. But the law also helped turn the reform into a revolution –a revolution which has serious effects even to the present day. Today's shortage of priest presiders for the Eucharist certainly can be attributed in part to the law of celibacy and ultimately to patriarchy. Because of celibacy we have fewer male eucharistic presiders; because of patriarchy and misogyny we have no female presiders.

The sacrament of ordination is a post-New Testament, historical development. As such, it is conditioned by the historical and cultural forces which were operative during its time of development. But this development never becomes an absolute as if it were a divine unchangeable law. All human developments in the Church are subject to continuing discernment. Do they still build up the Church? Or, have they become an obstacle to its mission to and in the world? Neglecting this discernment is a partial denial of the real presence of the Holy Spirit in the Church.

We come to this discernment with Christian detachment with the full knowledge that it may lead us to continue living the exception to what is human, or to embrace that which is fully human as a proper condition for effective ministry. Such discernment would normally be the fruit of the whole Christian community gathered in a Council or at least in a national synod.

At any rate, the theology of celibacy as it relates to the ministerial priesthood was never formally discussed before the subdeaconate. I accepted the law as a law of the Church, nothing more. It's quite possible to accept and obey the rules of the Church in the hope of receiving a reward in the next life or as a necessary institutional discipline. I suspect I accepted the celibacy law more as a price to be paid for the priesthood than as a witness to my single-hearted love for Christ, the eternal priest. For the younger readers, in those days before Vatican II, we were more conditioned to see Church law as God's will and to obey it without questions. The fact that there was hardly any theological or spiritual explanation just did not bother most of us. The law is the law.

In hindsight it is also strange that no one explained the tension, indeed, contradiction between a human law and our free acceptance of the gifts of the Holy Spirit. If chastity is a gift of the Spirit, we are free to accept or reject it. But rejecting the law meant a rejection of the priesthood.. It is also strange that St. Paul's counsel was never discussed: "concerning the unmarried. . .it is well for a person to remain as he is... But if you marry, you do not sin and if a girl marries she does not sin" (1 Cor. 7:25-28).

The law of celibacy takes effect in the sheltered environment of the seminary which is far removed from the actual conditions of the pastoral ministry. So, in an all male environment, celibacy is simply part of the artificial world closed in on itself. It is only when the seminarian passes out of this unreal world that his celibacy has to bear the stress and strain of serving both genders. Prayer and clinging to the risen Christ help the new priest to keep the law. But the law itself remains the product of a theology that emphasized suffering and penance as a means to gain salvation. If celibacy is a cross to be carried, then let it bring us closer to the suffering savior. When pressed, we could quickly find a rationale for celibacy. But it would be a rationale that could easily falter in a time of stress.

Theological Reflections

Having taught theology in a major seminary and in two Catholic Universities, I do not think there are any compelling reasons for seminarians to study their theology in the closed environment of a minor or major seminary. The theology I taught in the university was exactly the same as I taught in the major seminary. In fact, the theology in the university was enriched by the variety of down to earth questions posed by the students of both genders who live in the real world.

> I feel in our own time the seminary system has become obsolete. Seminaries for students studying for the priesthood were instituted as a response to the decrees of the Council of Trent.

(1545-1563). Trent's decree described the seminarians' course of studies as follows:

> "...they shall study grammar, singing, ecclesiastical computation and other useful arts; shall be instructed in Sacred Scripture, ecclesiastical books, the homilies of the saints, the manner of administering the sacraments, especially those things that seem adapted to the hearing of confessions, and the rites and ceremonies."[3]

It is easy to understand from the above course of studies:

> "That the intellectual training of candidates both here and abroad often left much to be desired,...The major emphasis in the seminaries was forming devout priests, rather than men of learning, and at Issy, the Sulpicians' seminary near Paris four hours were given over to intellectual work while the balance of the day was taken up with liturgical ceremonies, plain chant, visits to the Blessed Sacrament, benediction, recitation of the rosary, and other prayers."[4]

---

3 John Tracy Ellis, *The Catholic Priest in the United States*, (St. John's University Press, Collegeville, MN: 1971),12.

4 Ibid., 18.

It is a historical fact that the giants of theology have not been the products of seminary training in theology. St. Augustine, St. Albert the Great and St. Thomas Aquinas never attended a seminary. In our own time many of the leaders in theology are teaching in Catholic Universities, not in the seminaries. The seminary's physical isolation from the real world may protect the seminarians from exposure to the temptations of the world, but it does nothing to produce renowned intellectual leaders. If the seminary is meant to shelter the seminarian from the attractions of the world of two genders, it is indeed a poor preparation for actual pastoral ministry.

A New Approach To Preparation for the Priesthood

Today students wishing to study for the priesthood could go to a Catholic High School and then continue in a Catholic University which has a department of theology. They could take a core curriculum required and paid for by their bishop and participate regularly in the university's special formation program. This approach would have several advantages: First, students would be exposed to a much wider spectrum of theology. Second, they would live in the real world with the full spectrum of students they would serve after their ordination. Third, their formation for the priesthood would take place under real, down to earth conditions. Fourth, they would be tested in two semesters of field education under trained, competent supervisors. Fifth, in a mixed student body they would get a much better idea about the demands of the actual celibate life style. Each bishop would select the university for his students and receive the student evaluations as the years went on. The money saved by not having to maintain a separate seminary could be used to pay for the poor students' tuition. Seminarians, like other students, could also take jobs during the summer to earn their own room and board.

To return to my own story, while I was quite aware of the limitations of taking theology in the seminary, I was quite aware of the blessings of the celibate life style, like independence, freedom, and a simple life. For some unknown reasons I was always attracted to the simple life. Money or many possessions never appealed to me. If I could have a book to read, I was quite content. The vow of poverty taken by religious orders made a lot of sense to me. Even to this day I do not run to buy the latest new gadget on the market. Franciscan detachment brings with it a freedom to serve others. Service out of freedom is always better than service out of compulsion.

The call to serve in pastoral ministry is a continuing vocation. It provides meaning to the Christian life. One can hardly live under the name of Jesus Christ without a commitment to serve. The form of service is subject to continuing discernment since needs in whatever time and place vary considerably. For instance, today the Church and its ministers need to offer the ministry of hospitality to the growing number of immigrants who are hungry and poorly clothed. They are the strangers in our midst who need to be welcomed to join us in the breaking of the bread.

That celibacy would enable me to minister more effectively was fairly easy to understand. But it was not possible to foresee the emotional price that celibate life would exact as the years went on. The loneliness and the constant need to repress a God-given attraction to the opposite sex would take its toll. Ministering to women while keeping an emotional distance from them was never easy. Yet the celibacy law required a daily discipline which meant "being on guard" lest a natural attraction assert itself with such intensity as to dominate the attempt to minister. Over time such discipline could produce an unnatural, cold personality. Repressing a natural emotion is quite possible, with the help of God. But it can exact a heavy price. This price can be a daily offering to God. It can be part of the sacrifice required for effective ministry. But it can also become a heavy emotional burden during episodes of loneliness and depression. Bearing this burden alone never seems natural or normal. It may be a time when one needs a relationship so badly that any kind of sharing of the burden seems the rational thing to do. It is also a time when one is quite vulnerable to respond to any offer of help from the opposite sex.

With growing shortage of priest presiders we can hope that the next Ecumenical Council will repeal the celibacy law enacted for the Latin Rite by The Council of the Lateran in 1059. Today, Catholics have a much more positive view of sex. At the same time, the Church has made considerable progress in overcoming it's pathology of patriarchy and misogyny. The Church is quite ready for the full time ministry of women as eucharistic presiders. The time has come for the Church to recognize and bless what is a legitimate historical development.

In the meantime, the Church could consign the word "seminary" into it's ecclesiastical archives. The word itself is a symbol of a narrow approach to ministry, one which automatically excludes half the human race. Yet reading deeply into St. Paul's first letter to the Corinthians we are committed to being a Church which supports a diversity of ministries without regard to gender. If the purpose of an enclosed and isolated seminary is to protect the student from the opposite gender, it is, by definition, a poor and expensive preparation for serving both genders in actual ministry.

It is also a contradiction of the theology of diverse ministries which serve diverse needs in the life of an ever-changing Church. There is a blessed richness and openness to the Holy Spirit in the word "diversity." This is especially true when the word is linked to ministry. The body of the Church witnesses best to its own true identity when, within doctrinal boundaries, it reveals the flexibility of all living, growing bodies.

As the Church moves through the centuries, it needs to leave behind the structures which, due to the course of time or through fruitful historical developments, *have* become obsolete. (On the farm we eventually took the horse-drawn cultivator to the junk pile in the woods. The age of the tractor had arrived.) Of course, we have to overcome our emotional attachment to that which in fact is ready for burial. Clinging to that which does not build up the Church contradicts the Church's self-definition as a pilgrim Church: "the pilgrim church in her sacraments and institutions, which pertain to the present time, takes on the appearance of this passing world."[5] True pilgrims travel light. Like Cardinal Newman, they know "The night is dark, and I am far from home, Lead thou me on!"

---

5 *Dogmatic Constitution on the Church,* Walter J. Abbott, Ed. (New York: Herder and Herder, 1966), no. 48.

CHAPTER 3

Ordination to the Priesthood

The big day finally arrived! June 5, 1954! I was one of eight theology students who were ready for ordination to the priesthood for the Diocese of Lansing, Michigan. I was quite familiar with all the details of the ordination ceremony since I had seen it many times. The high point comes with the imposition of the bishop's hands. With this simple gesture I would become a priest forever according to the order of Melchizedech. Needless to say, it was a moment of great joy. It was the fulfillment of twelve years of prayer and hard study. To experience the fulfilment of such a long dream is emotionally almost overwhelming.

Yet the ordination event was full of mystery which was well beyond my understanding. It was a miracle unfolding before my very eyes. Mere human prayers and gestures could bestow the power to offer the Holy Liturgy. Only gradually did I internalize the full reality. That came with the celebration of my first Mass at St. Mary's Church in Westphalia, Michigan. It was another moment of awe and wonder no one can describe. The long lines of people seeking my first blessing was simply unforgettable. For some reason, I felt real close to my family who had been so distant while I was away for all those years in the seminary. From now on, I would wait for the bishop's appointment to a parish somewhere in the Diocese of Lansing, Michigan..

My appointment came rather quickly by phone the following Monday. I was being sent to The Church of the Resurrection in Lansing, Michigan. I would be an assistant to Msgr. John A. Gabriels of radio fame, at least around Lansing. I arrived with eager anticipation to begin my actual pastoral ministry. After twelve years of preparation and twelve years of dreaming about my life's ministry, I would finally enter the real world of priestly ministry.

Life in the Pastoral Ministry

I received a warm welcome by the pastor, Msgr. John A. Gabriels. My duties were gradually explained to me by the pastor and the other assistant. I would take turns with the other assistant in offering the daily Eucharist at 6:30 a.m. I would teach religion to the senior class in Resurrection High School next door. I enjoyed every minute of teaching the seniors. They were an attentive and, sometimes, challenging class. Every other day I would be in charge of answering the phone and the door. One could never know who or what would show up at that door.

Some days a man half drunk would show up and ask to take the pledge. It was a time to test my persuasive powers to get him to join Alcoholics Anonymous. Other times, a young couple would come to make arrangements for their upcoming marriage. Next, might come a husband or wife to make arrangements for the spouse's funeral. Other times, a couple might come for counseling before seeking a divorce. There were some Catholic lawyers who insisted the couples seeking divorce first take some counseling from their Catholic priests. Resurrection Parish was a large city parish. So the door and the phone were always busy. This was a great revelation to me.

I also had to take my turn teaching the convert class on Thursday evenings. In a large parish there were always people who wanted instructions in the Catholic Faith. Some were partners in an upcoming marriage; others simply wanted to join the Catholic Church. From the very first moment I enjoyed teaching this class. The questions were often so challenging that I would promise to address that issue in the next class, after more research. But the class often involved church history which I loved. It was always a moment of great joy to administer the sacrament of baptism to one of these new converts to the Faith.

After my second year at Resurrection I was appointed Athletic Director of Resurrection High School. This meant, among other things, that I had to ride the student bus to all the out of town football and basketball games. I had to sit in the back over the stinking motor to enforce discipline over the students. Often I would not get back to Lansing until 1:00 a.m. This was not fun on Saturday evenings when I had to get up to celebrate the six o'clock Mass on Sunday morning. It was hard to be fully prepared and awake for my own homily. The responsibility for the athletic program required endless fund-raising. This was an aspect of pastoral ministry which I endured only with reluctant obedience.

Resurrection Parish was responsible for chaplain duties for the nearby Sparrow Hospital. Again, I took turns with the other assistant in responding to the night calls to the emergency room to anoint the sick who had been in a car accident. The loss of sleep did not excuse me from teaching our High School class the next morning at 8:30 a.m. We also had to take Holy Communion to all the Catholics in the hospital.

The high point of each day was the celebration of the morning Liturgy. It was a wonderful way to start each day. Most of the time there were only a few parishioners in attendance. But this did not bother me. The celebration brought its own spiritual reward. I felt I was doing what a priest should be doing. Emotionally, I was always deeply involved in the Liturgy. It was and remains the heart of the Catholic Faith. Today's gradual loss of the Eucharist, due to the shortage of priest presiders, causes a deep sadness which is hard to overcome. Without the Eucharist our Church can no longer be called Church.

Life in the rectory was rather difficult since the housekeeper controlled the house. There was no secretary. So the other assistant and I had to fill out all the Mass cards for the sick and deceased. This consumed a good part of our time. There was, however, one rather pleasant part of life in the rectory and that was the day off. We could go golfing or go home to visit our parents. This was the only break from what gradually became a boring daily routine. Except for my teaching duties, there was nothing very challenging in the ministry. It seemed to be a rather repetitious administration of the sacraments. Hearing confessions on Saturdays soon became a monotonous duty. In the confessional there was really "nothing new under the sun."

Being a priest with a Roman collar did make a difference. I was always aware that the priesthood required a different life style. I became accustomed to daily prayer and to being available to serve the parishioners on a daily basis. Both the other assistant and I looked forward to our three week vacations. I often went canoeing with priest friends on the Pine River in Michigan. It was a great escape–a time to enjoy the song of the birds and the refreshing outdoors.

Flying

One day I had the day off and I was especially bored, even with golf. For reasons still unknown to me I was smitten with a great desire to explore flying. I remembered that even on the farm I had looked up wistfully at the single engine planes that flew overhead. I envied the pilots who were flying those mechanical birds around and above the clouds. Having spent many days on our farm tractor, I had considerable confidence in motors. I knew they did not just stop on their own unless there was something seriously wrong.

So it was with some confidence that I drove to the nearby airport in East Lansing and asked how much it cost to take flying lessons. The man behind the desk, who turned out to be the instructor, replied in a matter of fact fashion, that it would cost $10.00 an hour. The $10.00 included the cost of the plane rental and the instructor. I gave him the $10.00 and then and there we went out to a plane parked near the airport office. The first lesson consisted partly in explaining the parts of the airplane. This was a Piper J3, he explained. It had a 65 horse power engine. He explained the purpose of the aerilons on the wings which provided the turning power of the aircraft. Then he showed me the tail's rudders which went up and down and so put the plane in a downward or upward attitude. Finally, he showed me the oil and gas spouts. The gas spout had a wire sticking through the cap indicating the amount of fuel in the tank which was located directly in front of the pilot.

Then it was time to go up in the plane. Surprisingly he pointed me to the back seat while he went into the front seat. This small plane had only two seats, one in the front and the other in the back. Students always occupied the rear seat. Sitting in front, the instructor showed me the hand held accelerator under the left window. Then he showed me how to use the stick which came up between my legs. It controlled both the aerilons on the wings and the rudders on the tail. A movement to the left would turn the plane to the left; a movement to the right would turn the plane to the right. Pushing the stick forward would put the plane in a downward attitude; pulling it back would put the plane in a climbing mode. I felt it was all quite simple.

Now it was time to take off, with the instructor in the front and myself in the back. The instructor was at the controls and I was eagerly watching his every move. The little plane climbed off the runway with the motor at full power. (My instructor weighed at least 200 lbs. And that, I would learn a little later, made a big difference.) We went through various maneuvers in the air while he let me take over the controls. But he took over to show me the stall: he cut power and put the plane in a climbing attitude. Soon the plane started to fall. He applied power and we recovered quickly. But he explained what happens when the plane stalls in mid-flight. When we landed he asked when I would like to start formal instructions. I told him I would like to start next Wednesday since that was my only day off. He said, "Fine. Weather permitting, we will have your first flying lesson next Wednesday."

From then on, I eagerly watched the weather, especially on Wednesdays. But from then on all my days off were spent at the airport. After nine lessons the instructor announced that I was ready for my solo flight. He got out of the plane and gave me the "go" sign. I applied power and made my solo flight without much incident. My landing, however, was a bit nerve-racking since the plane did not descend at the usual rate. I pushed down harder on the stick and, of course, picked up speed. But fortunately, with good brakes, I brought the plane to a stop well before the end of the runway. It was only after I stopped that I figured out that, with the instructor missing, the plane was 200 lbs. lighter and naturally would float longer on the landing portion of the flight. It taught me the importance of weight and balance for the safety of the flight. It taught me to put all extra weight under the wings.

St. Luke

After four years at Resurrection Parish I was transferred to St. Luke Parish in Flint, Michigan. The ministry at St. Luke was mostly a repetition of the pastoral ministry at Resurrection. The big exception came when the pastor appointed me director of Friday's take-out fish fry. This was a fund raiser for the school. I had to gather volunteers to serve the fish and keep track of all the funds. It was administration pure and simple. As such, it was emotionally the most difficult part of my week. I could never adjust to this non-priestly duty.

Besides the fish fry I had to endure the pastor's pet dog. Of the two the fish fry was easier. The dog was not really house trained. So he used my office whenever he needed to take a pee. It reached a point where my office stunk like a dog's latrine. Finally, I had enough. When the pastor was on his annual vacation in Florida, I put the dog in the pastor's white Lincoln and took him to the Vet "to put him sleep." When I came back I reported to Mrs. O'Leary, the parish secretary, that I had put the "pastor's dog to sleep." She was delighted to hear the good news. Immediately she asked me how much it cost. I said: $10.00. She reached into the slush fund which we had for office expenses and gave me the $10.00. There was only one other person in the house who hated that dog more than I did and that was Mrs. O'Leary.

When the pastor came back, I reported what I had done to his pet dog. I expected a severe scolding. But he brushed it off with: "Well, he was getting old anyway." And that was the last we heard of that ugly mutt.

Most of my duties were the same every week, except here at St. Luke I had to teach religion to the eighth grade. Again, this was the fun part of my ministry. It was becoming clear to me that teaching was the most challenging and most rewarding part of my pastoral ministry.

I continued my flying lessons at a small airport nearby. My instructor was an 82 year old lady who needed a pillow to see outside. For $1200 I bought a used Taylorcraft which had the two seats next to each other. It was a high wing plane and so, except for the 65 horse engine, was quite different from the Piper J3 I was used to. But after a few take offs and landings my instructor gave me clearance to fly by myself. So from then on my days off were spent mostly in my Taylorcraft. But I still did not have a pilot's license permitting me to fly passengers.

After four years at St. Luke I was assigned as assistant to Msgr. Hardy at St. Mary's Church, Jackson Michigan. I knew this would be a difficult but short assignment. It was difficult because the pastor was an old time master of the house. My duties were mostly the same as at St. Luke. I had to teach the sophomore year in St. Mary's High School. That was a very pleasant escape from the rectory. Most of my duties at the rectory were confined to giving instructions to those wishing to join the Catholic Church. I also celebrated the a daily morning Mass, sometimes for the school children and, other times for the parishioners. The pastor was quite distant from his two assistants, so the other assistant and I shared our duties and our life in the rectory. Rectory life was rather routine.

The Second Vatican Council

However, the Second Vatican Council began in October of 1962. This was a great event in the Catholic Church. I read every word in the newspaper about this Council. For those of us who had studied the old text book theology, this Council was the most exciting event in the Church since I had been ordained. In fact, I would buy the *New York Times* to get more detailed reports. It was clear a new era was beginning in the Church. Even though it would be some years before the effects of the Council would reach the individual dioceses, it generated an enthusiasm for the coming future.

Pastor of St. James

After six months at St. Mary's I was, rather suddenly, assigned as pastor of St. James Parish in Mason, Michigan. It was an extremely cold January 12, 1963, when I backed my U-Haul to the rectory steps at St. James. The chancellor met me at the house and privately swore me in as the Administrator of the Parish. He said nothing about the suddenness of my assignment. He told me later that the less I knew the easier it would be to say: "I don't know" when questioned by the parishioners. But I soon discovered that the parishioners, through a very active grapevine, knew everything. The attempt at secrecy failed completely. In fact, it encouraged considerable embellishment of the actual facts.

This was a delicate assignment in the beginning since the previous pastor had been arrested for sexual abuse of small boys. According to a fairly reliable grapevine, the judge imposed the sentence that he leave Michigan and not return for seven years. So the bishop had sent him to some diocese in Texas. St. James was a more challenging assignment since I had full responsibility for everything going on in the parish.

My transfer to St. James happened within a day or two. From the viewpoint of administration, the parish was in a mess. In a small town such as Mason, the scandal of the pastor's sexual abuse had spread rapidly. It was my job to heal the wounds left by the previous pastor. It was a pleasant surprise to see how quickly the parishioners forgave the previous pastor and accepted me as his successor. I began my duties as a pastor and soon the people rallied around me. In my first year I made only minor changes. I felt a great need to wait for the parishioners to support me and my ministry. With my arrival the Sunday collection increased. So I paid off part of the debt to the Cathedral in Lansing. There was a great need for a rectory, but I felt the time was not ripe for such a move. So I just lived in a small, ordinary house.

I did start a Parish Pastoral Council which was an implicit recommendation of the Second Vatican Council, then in session in Rome. A Parish Council was totally new in traditional parish administration. But I enjoyed every minute. It meant that lay people elected by the parishioners would meet with me once a month to discuss parish policy. It became especially important in implementing the many changes ordered by Vatican II. I made no changes unless first approved by the new council. This experience with the Pastoral Council would have a lasting effect on my relationship with the parish as an ecclesial unit in the church. Years later, I would publish five books on Parish Pastoral Councils. One would sell 20,000 copies.

One evening I was in the Parish Hall teaching a class of adults for the Diocese of Lansing. It turned out to be a life-changing evening. After one class Dr. Bergeon's wife came up to me and, looking me straight in the eye, said: "You should be a teacher. You make things so clear." She was a graduate of Marygrove and I knew she did not say things like this without considerable thought. At any rate, I did not sleep that night, mulling over her words over and over. From that night on, I dreamed of becoming a teacher. The priesthood would be one way of obtaining that goal.

With my appointment to the parish came a second appointment as chaplain to the Lansing Boys Training School. This was in fact a reform school. I was in charge of the Catholic boys while a Protestant Minister was in charge of the Protestant boys. It meant that I had to spend at least two full days at the school each week. My day was filled with counseling the delinquent boys in the hope of getting them first to repent of raping and, sometimes, killing the girl. Secondly, I tried to get them to turn a new leaf, relying on the grace of their Catholic Faith. At times this job seemed hopeless. Most of the boys, upon their release, fell into the same routine of stealing cars, raping or breaking into homes. In fact, many of the boys, after a second or third offense, would end up in jail in Mason which was also my responsibility.

As chaplain, I had access to all my boys' records. It was enlightening to read all about their home background. It was a revelation to see how many boys came from broken homes, either due to divorce or alcohol. I could not help but feel sorry for these boys who often were caught up in the gangs of Detroit. The gangs became their home. Under the influence of these gangs the boys easily fell into a life of crime. Driving back to Mason at the end of the day, I often wondered if I would have done any better if I had been born and raised under similar conditions.

There was the tendency to blame society or the parents. But that was too simplistic. I did a lot of reading about delinquent boys. But at the end, I decided there was no single answer. But negligent parents often seemed to be to blame. They had no preparation for training and educating their own children. The greatest responsibility of marriage and parenting was simply ignored. It was amazing how many men and women entered marriage without a thought about preparation for training their children. Parents are the childrens' first teachers and it is clear they often fail miserably. The Reform School could hardly replace the role of the parents. So my work at the Reform School was very discouraging. In spite of the staff's obvious dedication, success in truly reforming a young man was rare indeed. Recidivism seemed to be the norm. Instead of taking the road to real reform, most of the boys clung to their conviction: "Next time I won't get caught." I concluded that a rather deep faith has to be the foundation for true repentance. And that kind of faith was usually missing.

The beginnings of an answer, it seems to me, has to come with more adult education in the parishes and community colleges. The curriculum would include courses in religious morality, elementary psychology and the basic principles of education. After reading the background reports of hundreds of my students over a four year period, I became convinced that every couple planning to marry should be required to attend a full day workshop on parenting. The future father and mother would learn the importance of loving presence in their family home. This would hardly be a cure-all, but it would go a long way to keep their children from going astray.

The Second Vatican Council, with all its recommended changes, ended in 1965. The Council was the greatest event in my life. It meant the Church was alive and capable of change and adjustments to real parish life. I fell in love with the changing Church. Now it was time to implement all those changes throughout the Diocese of Lansing. To my surprise, Bishop Zaleski called me to his office to explain that I would be in charge of implementing the teachings of Vatican II throughout the diocese. Then he added rather casually that I would have to give up my parish. This new job would be full-time.

This appointment was a great surprise. I had no special education in theology or any other degrees. But I was delighted to accept the appointment even though I had to give up the parish. I moved over to St. Vincent Orphanage in Lansing. I lived with another priest, Fr. Francis Murray, who was a dear friend of mine. He was in charge of Catholic Social Service Office. So my living conditions were ideal for the job I was given.

Renewal Through Vatican II

I threw myself into this new job with great excitement. I selected a committee with diocesan-wide representation. We met monthly and decided on a three level approach to educating the Diocese of Lansing in the sixteen documents of Vatican II. The first level would be discussion clubs in the home; the second level would be adult education classes in each deanery; the third level would be three-day workshops at the retreat house to train those who would be in charge of educating all adults in their respective deaneries.

On the organizational level, I asked the pastors of the parishes to choose a lay chairperson for their own parish programs. Each deanery also had a director who served on the diocesan board. The deanery director had to come to our workshops at the retreat house. There we explained all the materials and the methods to be used throughout the diocese.

One of our first decisions was to select the most important of the 16 Vatican II documents and prepare discussion booklets. We were able to get two competent laypersons from the Office of Education to prepare discussion booklets for the whole diocese. The booklets were written in language the average lay person could understand. They were well received throughout the diocese. They became the key to reaching the grassroots people.

I went to all the deanery meetings to provide an overall view of the whole program. Since at that time the diocese had 10 large counties, I was on the road most of the time. I felt like a salesman for Vatican II. All this was fine with me since, like our bishop, I was convinced that Vatican II was the greatest event of our lifetime. It was a Council which gave us a totally new approach to ecclesiology which is my favorite subject.

The program continued for three years. Toward the end of the second year I wrote a letter to all the pastors asking them to implement the teaching of *The Dogmatic Constitution on the Church* and start a parish council. Since I had a very successful experience with such a council in my parish in Mason, Michigan, I assumed, incorrectly, that pastors would be happy to start such a council.

Soon after the letter went out the bishop called me in and gave me a mild scolding for not checking with him before I sent out such a letter. Driving back home that night I felt the bishop was 100% correct. After some thought, it was understandable that he would prefer to send out such a letter himself. But that was the only time that the bishop inserted himself into our program. He was a man who gave considerable latitude to those he appointed to diocesan jobs. But my letter was not a major problem. Some pastors started a council and others did not. Either way was O.K. with me.

One day I was in my office preparing to conduct a workshop on Parish Pastoral Councils when a stranger appeared at my door. He introduced himself as Neil Kluepfel. He said he had worked for *Our Sunday Visitor* but was now on his way to Mystic, Conn. to start a Catholic Magazine to be called *Today's Parish*. He asked me to write a monthly column on Parish Councils. I had been writing a weekly column for our own Lansing Diocesan Newspaper, but I was quite surprised and honored to be invited to write for a national magazine.

I accepted Neil's gracious invitation and began writing a Question and Answer column almost immediately. I got most of my questions at workshops I was conducting on Parish Councils. But I discovered that I really looked forward to writing that monthly column. I would write and re-write until I was satisfied with the final product. This column basically began my writing career. Twenty-third Publications put some of my columns together and published two books on Parish Councils. Later Twenty-Third Publications published two of my *Guides* for Parish Councils which were widely used throughout the U.S. and Canada. In those days few pastors knew anything about Parish Councils. So my *Guides* received a warm welcome. No doubt the *Guides* were a large factor in the invitations I received to conduct over 350 workshops on Parish Pastoral Councils in the U.S. and Canada.

In the third year of this program I received an invitation to conduct a retreat for the Maryknoll priests in Seoul, South Korea. They wanted a retreat that would focus on the theology of Vatican II. Somehow they had heard of our program in the Diocese of Lansing. I advised the Maryknoll Director that I could conduct a retreat during the summer months when I was not busy with our Lansing Program. They accepted the date of June, 1967.

So it was that I found myself on a thirteen hour flight to Tokyo by way of Alaska. I took a Chinese airline to Seoul, South Korea. I conducted three retreats since the Maryknoll house could not house all the Maryknoll priests in South Korea at one time. I asked the priests to form small groups to discuss how the new theology of Vatican II applied to South Korea. This was departure from the usual lecture method. But it was well received by the missionaries. And I was delighted by the100% participation. It was the first and only time that I gave a retreat. At that time, I had no problems with my voice. That would come later.

When I finished the retreat, I flew home by way of Hong Kong and New Delhi, India. I took a day off to visit the Taj Mahal which certainly merits being one of the seven wonders of the world. It was hard to leave. But I went on to Beirut, Rome and New York. I was on a flight around the world, but I spent most of the time in the air. I was actually quite pleased to land in New York. It would be only one more day to Michigan. It was time to get back to directing the Renewal Program for the Diocese of Lansing.

After running the program for three years the bishop decided to let the office of education continue the program. It was a precious moment for me. I decided to ask permission to go away to study theology and earn a Masters degree in Theology. This was especially important at this time, it seemed to me, since Vatican II produced a large body of new theology. To my delight the bishop gave his O.K. on the spot. He let me choose the university. So I told him I would like to go to St. John's University, conducted by the Benedictines in Collegeville, MN. The bishop graciously gave his consent and paid for all my room, board and tuition.

Back to School

It was a moment of great joy as I loaded my U-haul and drove to Collegeville, MN. To avoid Chicago, I decided to take the ferry from Muskegon to Milwaukee. It was a smooth ride on Lake Michigan. I enjoyed every minute. With my arrival in Collegeville I was assigned a room and presented with my course of studies leading to the Masters Degree. I took nine credits during the regular semester and six during the summer semester.

Even though I had been away from school for fourteen years, it was good to get "back to the books." All the professors were excellent. They were well in tune with all the changes coming to theology from Vatican II. They inspired a love for the new theology in all the students. For me, it was a pleasant discovery to see that theology had moved from the largely static form which I had studied in the seminary in the early 50's to a more dynamic pastoral style. It was fun to do all the required readings and to write the required papers.

The final paper, which was rather long, was the greatest challenge. But it was enjoyable to pursue a particular topic in greater depth. I was scheduled to finish my Masters Degree at the end of the fall semester in 1968. But, rather suddenly, word came from my bishop that I was to continue my studies to obtain the doctorate. This was a great surprise to me.

It seems, according to a fairly reliable grapevine, that some of the professors at St. John's Provincial Seminary in Michigan had signed Fr. Charles Curran's letter objecting to Pope Paul VI's encyclical on birth control published in 1968. So the bishops felt they had to terminate their contract with the Sulpician professors of theology at St. John Seminary. So their own seminary had no professors. If the seminary was going to continue, the bishops had to find some qualified professors. So it was only natural that the bishop would ask me to go on for the doctorate so that I would be qualified to teach at their Michigan seminary.

Again, my bishop let me select the university I liked to continue my studies. I took my final six credits at St. John's university. I received my Masters degree and immediately enrolled at Aquinas Institute then located at Dubuque, Iowa. I considered other universities, but my mother was ill at that time and I thought I should stay close to home for visits. The bishop accepted my choice.

Aquinas Institute specialized in theology. So there was a rather small student body. And each class was also small. Each student was given special attention. And, again the professors were excellent. I had no problem with any member of the faculty. They were Dominicans thoroughly dedicated to theology. And, I have to admit, their dedication was contagious.

I began my studies at Aquinas in the fall of 1969. With such a small student body, we all felt like family. In the dining room the faculty routinely ate with us. We soon got to know most everybody in the school. There were no rules that I can remember. It was assumed we would act like adults. I thoroughly enjoyed the small classes. Again, I plunged myself into my studies with zeal and excitement.

In 1972 I received a surprise phone call from Fr. Rose, the rector of St. John's Provincial Seminary in Michigan. He advised me that the deacon class, soon to be ordained, had not yet had a course in Christology. Would I please come and teach Christology for the spring semester? I was only a doctoral candidate at that time, but fortunately I was quite ready to teach such a course. The rector had already received my bishop's O.K. for the move.

Of course, I felt quite honored to be invited to teach a course which was in fact in my area of specialization. I agreed to come to the Seminary to teach, even though I did not yet have my doctorate. But I closed the book on my dissertation at Aquinas and took off for the seminary in Michigan. It was quite a joy to teach Christology to the deacons. In a sense it was an ideal teaching environment. To a man the deacons were deeply interested in Christology and I had their attention from the first minute of class. The class confirmed what I had suspected all along, namely, that I would enjoy teaching. The curriculum committee compressed the class into nine weeks so I would not lose too much time writing my dissertation.

After completing the six week Christology course, I drove back to Dubuque to continue working on my dissertation. The title of my dissertation was: "An evaluation of the teaching on Episcopacy in Chapter Three of Vatican II's Constitution on the Church." One problem I had from the beginning was the lack of theological works on the theology of Vatican II. Not enough time had elapsed since the close of the Council for theologians to publish any in-depth analysis of the Vatican II documents. So far as sources were concerned I mostly had to go it alone. But my director came to the rescue by recommending I limit my research by using the documents themselves. So with his encouragement I was quite secure in moving forward with my evaluation. I was able to concentrate on Vatican II's *Dogmatic Constitution on the Church.*

While concentrating on a dissertation I felt like I had become a monk for a year or more. I was blessed since both my bishop and the seminary faculty gave me the time and space to continue my work. So within a year, I had finished the dissertation and was ready for the big day called the Defense of my doctoral thesis. I got word from Aquinas that my defense would be at the end of December 1973. Since I had returned to teaching at the Seminary, I had very little time to prepare for my Defense.

On my drive to Dubuque I hit quite a snow storm going through Indiana. I stopped at the first motel I could find through the blinding snow. The next day I arrived at Aquinas ready for the Defense. All five members of the board had received copies of my dissertation and were quite ready with a barrage of questions. But all in all, the Defense went well. I was given a pass. My director congratulated me and took me out to dinner to celebrate. The diploma attesting to the Ph.D. in Theology came a few days later through the mail. It was a high point in my life.

St. John's Provincial Seminary

I returned the next day to Plymouth, Michigan, to teach at St. John Provincial Seminary.

Teaching at a Seminary is fairly simple. The program of courses for each of the four years follows the standard outline for all Major Seminaries. There are few electives. The students, as can be expected, are well behaved and intensely interested in their subjects. At that time there were few women enrolled. Some were going for an M.Div. Degree to become Directors of Religious Education in the parish. I had to be an academic advisor to only a few students, since I was the Director of the Deacon Program.

So, I had to prepare Deacon Workshops. Besides giving lectures myself, I had to contact outside speakers who basically picked some specialty that normally came under the list of Deacon Duties. Training the priest-supervisors was the most challenging part of the job. Priests were not used to being evaluated for their ministry. Yet, if a deacon was assigned to a parish, the pastor was expected to meet weekly with his deacon to conduct an evaluation of the week's ministry. So, I had to prepare a list of questions and a guideline for this evaluation. The deacon has to get a passing grade in his deacon internship to be admitted to the priesthood.

Besides occasional golf, I did allow myself one childish distraction from the sometimes boring, seminary routine. I bought a small 250 cc. motorcycle. Actually it was too small, as I soon experienced when a 18 wheeler went by. The after-draft pulled by motorcycle so much I thought I was going to go off the road. But it was also too small for ordinary crosswinds. I had to hang on for dear life. Otherwise, it was fun to take the inter-state to Toledo. The fresh air was also a delightful departure from the "cloister" of the seminary.

One of the high points of my motorcycle life came when I gave Sister Claudia, our aging librarian, her first motorcycle ride. Actually, the thrill of riding a motorcycle wore off rather quickly. Two serious spills onto the roadway diminished the thrill considerably. After a year I decided I had passed my male mid-life crisis and so I sold my little toy.

I had been teaching at St. John Seminary for four years when I received a surprise phone call from Gonzaga University in Spokane, WA. This very famous Jesuit university was offering me the Flannery Chair in Roman Catholic Theology. From the beginning I was inclined to accept such a generous offer. I had to ask permission from my bishop. With his usual sense of humor the bishop said: "If some one offers an old man like you a chair, you ought to accept it." And so I did. I would occupy the chair for one year beginning in September, 1977.

Once again I loaded my U-Haul with my earthly possessions and headed West. This time I decided to drive around the Chicago traffic. Arriving in Spokane, I rented an apartment near the university Almost at the same time, I explored the possibility of serving as chaplain to a sisters' monastery. Again, luck was with me. I was invited to live in the chaplain's quarters at the Convent of the Sisters of the Holy Name. This was a great blessing since the sisters did both the cooking and the cleaning. I did not have to pay for an apartment.

I began my teaching at Gonzaga in the fall of 1977. The Jesuits received me warmly and invited me to all their faculty gatherings. They treated me as one of their own. Indeed, I felt I belonged there. I have been in awe of the Jesuits ever since. They are simply amazing. They really know how to run a university. Our student body came from the whole world. The Jesuits granted scholarships to students as far away as Vietnam.

Since I held the Flannery Chair, I was expected to produce a scholarly work worthy of publication. But I did not have to attend any meetings. So, I decided to explore the theology of the Catholic parish. In March of 1978 I delivered my Flannery lecture to the whole faculty and student body. It was the high point of my theological career. In fact, the faculty invited me to stay on to teach on the Gonzaga faculty the following year. This was another wonderful opportunity which I just had to accept. Once again the bishop gave his approval.

I kept up my flying habits as a very pleasant distraction, In fact, three of us bought a used Cessna 172 and signed up to use it as we had time. It actually helped me in one teaching assignment to Richland, WA., about 130 miles Southwest of Spokane. I had to teach a ten week course in the evening hours. I flew myself to the airport in Richland and a student picked me up to take me to class. I slept at the rectory and in the morning the pastor took me to the airport. By 11:00 a.m I was back in my class at Gonzaga.

I had one scary moment, however, at the airport at Coeur d' Alene, Id. I enjoyed flying around the lake, but one day I was a bit distracted as the tower announced the wind direction for landing. And foolishly I did not ask for a repeat. A strong crosswind gust got under may left wing and lifted it to the point where my right wing came within three inches of ground. I saved the day with a hard left on the aerilons to straighten out my wings. But it was the last time that I landed without clearly understanding the tower's directions.

After spending a summer in Michigan I returned to teach at Gonzaga. But at that time I was still committed to conducting workshops on Parish Pastoral Councils. So sometimes, I gave a workshop on the weekend and took my place in the classroom on Monday morning. This amounted to a lot of teaching in a short space of time. I continued this schedule at Gonzaga for four years. But this heavy schedule took its toll.

With my constant battle with allergies, I ended up losing my voice. The doctor shined his light into my throat and then made his pronouncement: "If you expect to teach again, you have to shut up for a year and give your voice a real rest." This was a serious emotional blow. ("How do I pay the rent?" I said to myself. By this time I was actually living in an apartment near the university.)

As I was leaving the doctor's office, I saw a Tour Bus drive by. "That bus driver doesn't have to talk," I said to myself. I went immediately to the office of the bus company. "Do you need a bus driver?" I asked the man behind the desk. "As a matter of fact, we do." He responded. I could apply, he said, but I had to pass three tests: a physical, a written and a road test. I passed all three tests in a few days. Within a week I received a call to take a bus load of high school students to Seattle. Going to Seattle on my first drive was uneventful. This first time the roads were excellent.

But driving back, I thought I heard some singing in the back of the bus. I listened as the song became louder: "We want to wee, wee. We want to wee, wee." I lost no time finding a McDonald's. My bus load lined up in front of the bath room while I got a free egg McMuffin.

In due time we hit the road again to return to Spokane.

The next ride to Seattle was quite scary. I hit an ice patch passing through the Cascade mountains. I had to slow down to fifteen miles an hour for about fifteen miles. I could hear the grumbling in the bus, but we got through the ice without incident. The next encounter with ice came when I was returning from Pullman to Spokane. I had a full bus load and, coming over a hill, my headlights fell upon a sheet of ice– all down hill. I could not slow down and there was an accident at the bottom of the hill. Resisting the urge to brake, my heavy bus picked up speed going down hill. I eased over to the left lane to pass the accident. My full bus gained speed. I flew fast the accident at about 65 miles an hour. Fortunately, I missed the accident and soon was able to slow down going uphill. How happy I was to get back to the station in Spokane without incident! God and His angels were with us that day.

But I was quite pleased when my year of bus driving was over. Assuming my voice could carry a full load of teaching, I went back to Gonzaga University to return to my job. However, I was told that my position had been filled and there was no opening for at least a year. So after a few weeks to ponder my situation, I decided to take a year off to work in the Mexican American Apostolate in Brownsville, TX. I ended up at St. Luke Parish in Brownsville. I enrolled in evening classes in Spanish and eventually, I was able to preach in Spanish and work in the office with both English and Spanish parishioners.

Soon, I started making my regular visits to the Mexican barrio that was outside of the city limits in the poor part of the county. Normally, I had to park my car outside of the actual barrio since there was no real road into the barrio. There was no drainage system. So after a rain, I had to trudge through the water standing all over or running over the entrance lane.

I made a habit of visiting the sick. Normally, I had a bunch of children following me to the sick. They knew who in the barrio was sick and were glad to lead me to that house trailer. The sick had no health insurance so their supply of drugs was always in need of a refill. It was hard to find transportation since most of the old cars in the barrio were not working.

We always gathered under the children's favorite tree to give instructions to those who were preparing for their first Holy Communion. The children sat on the ground and, in general, were deeply grateful that I was coming to them. After all, they had no way to get to our catechetical instructions which were held in the school well into the city of Brownsville. When the day of First Communion arrived I received many invitations to dinner in the barrio. I was delighted to pick the poorest family and share in a Mexican cooked chicken dinner with really hot habaneros and jalapenos. My stomach protested for three days. But it was wonderful to accept the gracious hospitality of the poor. For some reason, I had the distinct feeling that "I belong here."

There is a great difference between taking up a collection for the poor during the Mass on Sunday and actually living with the poor, however briefly. I began to wonder what it would be like if all Catholics could have a real experience living with the poor. It would be wonderful to build an actual church of the poor with the celebration of the Liturgy under the children's favorite tree. Many times "mere" presence is the greatest gift we can give to the poor. The New Testament often calls Christians to offer hospitality to the strangers. (Rom. 12:13, 1 Tim. 3:2; Tit:1-8, 1 Pet. 4:9). Unfortunately, in many parishes the poor remain strangers.

My work in Brownsville let me have a break now and then to go to South Padre Island, the finest oasis on this spinning globe. I enjoyed jogging along the beach and just meditating in the midst of the birds and the waves. The beach was restful and invigorating at the same time.

After a year in Brownsville I felt a great need to get back to teaching theology. I saw an ad in a Catholic Newspaper for a professor of theology at Duquesne University, Pittsburgh, PA. I updated my resume and sent it to Duquesne. Within a few days I received a call to be interviewed. My interview went quite well. And within the same day I got word that I was hired. It meant that I would teach theology and, at the same time, serve as Director of the Masters Degree Program in Pastoral Ministry. After my year in the Mexican American Apostolate, I felt quite ready to get back to teaching pastoral theology.

Life at Duquesne University

Moving to Pittsburgh with a U-Haul was no problem. I managed to get an apartment not far from the university. I was the director of the Masters Degree program so I had only a two-third teaching load, including both graduate and undergraduate students. I plunged into my teaching duties with great delight. It was quite relief from my boring bus driving. Most of my students in the Masters Degree program were adults who hoped to get hired in a parish as director of Religious Education or something similar. The Program grew as the diocese of Pittsburgh insisted on a Masters degree for all directors. So at one time I had over 60 students in the M.A. program.

They were the "cream of the crop." It was a great privilege to have them in the program. I worked with a wonderful priest in Pittsburgh who was in charge of training all the catechetical directors. He gladly accepted all the university's requirements for either the eighteen credit certificate or the 30 credit degree. I was delighted to be of service to the Diocese of Pittsburgh since I always wanted theology to have good roots in the actual pastoral experience of the Church.

One of the features of the program I really liked was the required six credit field experience. This meant that all my students had to serve as interns in a parish for two semesters. They had to come to the university once a month for our theological reflection sessions. During these sessions we used the case study method and the critical incident method. Both worked rather well to bring the reflections from the classroom to the real pastoral life of the Church.

One of the blessed by-products of this system was that my students had no problem finding a job once they had their degree. Their competence was well known in the diocese. With the growing shortage of priests, pastors were glad to hire trained supervisors of their religious education programs. In short, I was happy that both my experience and my training could benefit the diocesan church. My seven years at Duquesne University were a perfect fit for me.

However, after seven years the administrative details of the Masters Program were getting to my health. So unfortunately, I had to resign my position when I reached 65. I had hoped to get rid of the administration, but that didn't work. The job description for this position included the requirement to direct the Masters Degree program.

So it was with a great deal of sadness that I handed in my resignation. It was readily accepted since both the dean and the faculty knew about the frailty of my age and health. But in my heart I knew that I could still teach a class and do a good job. Besides that, I always had a dream to do more writing. My love for writing never left me. So, as I was driving back from Duquesne I was sure that reaching sixty-five did not mean I could no longer teach. Sixty-five is a rather arbitrary figure for retirement. My competence in teaching did not vanish just because I reached a certain age. Nevertheless, my life at Duquesne came to an end. I would have to find other ways to teach and write.

CHAPTER 4
Falling in Love

Everything humanly possible has been said, sung or written about "love." Or, so they say. But I have my doubts. We humans continue to stumble for words and symbols to express what in our heart of hearts can't be expressed. Every day we encounter mysteries which are beyond our finite understanding. We may get a passing glimpse of a few of the mysteries that surround us. Both our reason and our emotions can bend to the breaking point; but the mystery of love always wins. It remains unscathed. It floats upward and outward, waiting for another day. Humans bracket their lives with calendars of days and months; but the mystery of love will not be so bound. It is beyond human clocks and calendars.

But true love is also a power. It clings to us in a hundred ways. It can be so powerful that we are ready to lay down our lives for the one we love. This kind of love is a forerunner and foundation for loving the risen Christ through the ups and downs of the workaday world. But it remains a human love. It is a full engagement of all our human resources. Through this engagement our love expresses itself in compassion, in sympathy, in offering our helping hand. Thus love is the power that creates a new self and a new world.

Love is a mystery that won't be subdued. It will not be contained or described by human words, symbols or emotions. Only when we say, "God is love" do we get a passing glimpse. We get a glimpse of the infinite God and His infinite love. But, in an instant, it's gone. It has vanished into eternity. Our finite capacity to comprehend love has been tested and found wanting.

For love, if it is a truly human love, is a marriage between reason and emotion. How they come together remains beyond our frail human understanding. We have God-given freedom to repress both our emotions and our human reason. But love will not really be repressed. It waits patiently for another day. Then it may erupt beyond the boundaries of human reason. Even though theoretically human reason remains the master, it will at times yield to the mystery that is love. All this means that even human reason does not always remain in charge. At the end of the day, no matter how intense the struggle, the mystery of love will remain the winner.

The book of Genesis gives us a glimpse, but only a glimpse, of love as a mysterious relationship between two genders. Amazingly, the two genders remain unique even though they are created to be in relationship with each other. One may deny or repress one's attraction for the other gender, but it will always persist. All denials will fall victim to the revealed truth of the persistence of the divinely created relationship. Denial simply places the denying human in an unreal world. Denial may win a passing victory, but eventually the real world of two genders making a relationship human will win the day. "God saw all that He had made, and indeed it was very good." (Gen. 1:31.)

From the moment of creation we are destined to be a social animal, to live in a community of humans. Community is a natural form of the human condition. Growth will be in some form of community or there will be no growth. The single life will forever remain the exception. The relationship with God points both to human origin and to human destiny. We came from the Creator and do best if we remain fixed on the final return to Him. We have a divine destiny whether we acknowledge it or not.

To be human, then, is to be in relationship with that other who makes up the human. Without that other we fail as a partner completing the human. Without God as our divine other our image as truly human also fails us. The creator designed us to be human through two healthy relationships, one with Himself and one with an other human. Of course, we are free to repress our inner nature's deep longing for those two relationships, both the human and the divine. But in doing so, we are no longer truly human as created in God's image. Our humanity is flawed.

Another possibility is that love can override reason. When our actions are separated from reason, we can perform actions which we deeply regret once reason reasserts itself. This can happen with any emotion, but is especially serious in the case of love. To abdicate one's reason is another way of being less than fully human. To abdicate one's reason in favor of love is to abandon one's responsibility both to self and to human society.

All the above can be found in a any good book on Christian anthropology. But at Duquesne University in 1992 I was not quite ready for this book knowledge to pass into my daily life. I was quite aware that there was an emptiness in my daily life which could not be filled merely by doubling my prayers and nourishing my spiritual life. I had tried that without success.

A Ride to Duquesne?

That day in early September began with the usual routine. I celebrated the morning Liturgy in the chapel where I was assigned as chaplain while teaching at Duquesne University. I was having breakfast with the sisters when one of the sisters came up to me. She asked me if I would mind taking along a Duquesne student on my way to the University. Without much thought I said: "That's fine with me." Then sister told me the student would meet me at my car in the parking lot in the back of the Convent.

Arriving at my car after breakfast, a young lady was waiting for me. I invited her to step into my car and, after a brief introduction, we were on our way to Duquesne. She turned out to be a graduate student and, therefore, a little older than most students. We had time only for very brief conversation before we arrived at Duquesne. As she was leaving, she asked if she could get a ride back at the end of the work day, at about 5:00. p.m. Again, without further thought, I said:"Sure."

That's how it all began. Mary[6] became my regular rider to the university. We exchanged light conversation to and from. But one day I discovered it was her birthday and so I invited her out to an Italian restaurant to celebrate. We had a long and very enjoyable conversation. My reason knew it was wrong for a professor and priest to take a student out on a date. But it was a case when my love was overriding my reason. For a brief time my love had banished my reason to some never-never land. I took Mary back to the rented rooms at the convent and simply asked if she had class in the morning. When she said yes, I told her I would be happy to pick her up at the usual time. And so it went.

---

6 "Mary" is a fictitious name.

When she did not work or have class, I really missed her presence in the car. She was a gentle soul but quite an intellectual, as I discovered. I confess I had never been that comfortable with any lady before. So I found myself thinking about her during the day. I looked forward to picking her up on the way home. It was some time before I came to the realization that I was really in love with Mary. She was more than a companion to and from work. She was constantly present to me in my imagination. It was wonderful that I sensed she was also in love with me. Ours was not a one way relationship. The attraction to the opposite gender that I had repressed so long suddenly was alive and well.

Upon reflection I decided one does not so much "fall" in love as grow into it gradually. On the level of feeling, it seemed quite natural that she cared a lot for me and that I cared a lot for her. The routine kiss at end of the ride seemed like a normal good bye. She was not pushing me and I was not pushing her.

But the phrase, "Falling in love" did convey part of the truth. Since the emotion of love seemed, at times, to take over, I had the sensation of falling. When reason is no longer in charge, one does lose the stability which reason provides. So under the power of the emotion of love, my life, it seemed, was no longer my own. This was a unique sensation, but it revealed only part of my experience. My reason would sometimes interject itself into the process to prove that the emotion of love did not really have total control. So my days were filled with a mix of reason and emotion.

It was only a matter of time until Mary and I found ourselves playing tennis at a nearby park. Since she was not an aggressive lady, I was always quite comfortable with her. Our relationship grew almost unconsciously. In the meantime, I had to ask myself if I was falling in love. I could not help but answer in the affirmative. Until then, I never discussed my relationship with her. But I could no longer deny my emotional attachment. I had to admit it was love. After living a single life for so many years, it was a gradual surprise to discover how vulnerable I was to her love. She was present in my imagination and in my soul. Her love breathed life and energy into all my emotions. Every drop of my blood, it seemed, was now running for her.

It was just a matter of time until I asked her to help me in writing a book. I was never much good at the typewriter or at the computer. She graciously agreed. Her computer skills were out of this world, so far as I was concerned. So I ended up dictating the whole book to her while she made my computer jump and bounce like it was a toy. I did a lot of preparation for my dictation, but it all worked rather well. She was a God-send. The book went off to the publisher and I received an acceptance call within a few days.

After a year of enjoying the love of this relationship, Mary suddenly decided to terminate our relationship. I never did understand exactly why, but she mentioned our age gap which was almost thirty years. But for me it was enough that she wanted to end our relationship. I did not want to impose myself on her in any way. I had enough respect for her that I respected her decision even though I did not understand all the reasons.

But ending such a close relationship was not easy. She continued to be present in my imagination for many months. In fact, the love between us was so deep and so all-embracing that I was sure I would never again experience that kind of love. To this day, I have never fallen in love with the intensity similar to that which I experienced with Mary.

But I had one escape. I could always plunge deeper into theology which, strange as it may seem, can also be an all-embracing love. Naturally, it is an intellectual love which, to some extent, by-passes or over-rides the human emotions. But one can deliberately get lost in theology, knowing that, in the mean time, one has to repress the emotional side of one's life. But I still feel sorry for people who have never had a love experience like mine.

Love is a rich dimension of this life's journey. Without it one has a lonely journey indeed.

The human relationship that is love teaches us that life is meant to be shared, that life is fully human only in relationship with another human. Ultimately, this sharing leads to community. For all humans are designed by the all wise creator to be in relationship. That will forever be the road to growth and happiness. It will also be an important part of life's journey. But life can and does go on without it. But after my break-up with Mary I knew what is meant by "falling" in love. One can indeed recover from a fall. But the rest of the journey will never be the same. The wound remains.

Love is also a great teacher. Once I knew how much Mary loved me, yes, "ignoble" me, it was much easier to understand that a forgiving God could also love me and love me for all eternity. The experience of being loved opens new doors. It shows us that love is not just an abstract word that may have meaning some day in the future. If the creator could create this kind of all embracing love, how much more anxious would this Creator be to embrace me with his eternal love.

Retirement

After seven years at Duquesne, I celebrated my sixty-fifth birthday. Retirement was not compulsory, but the administrative details of directing a Masters Degree program were eating away at my health. I still enjoyed teaching, but I did have a dream to write books when I retired. So in May of 1993 I wrote my letter of resignation to the Dean of the University. At the same time, I wrote a letter to my bishop in Lansing, asking to retire from the active priesthood. I quickly received letters accepting my resignation both from the University and from the priesthood.

Retiring from the priesthood was quite difficult even though I had hopes of teaching in Southern Texas where there was no Catholic University. On the other hand, on the level of feeling, the priesthood had, over time, gradually left me. Since teaching occupied all my time, I had no time for the traditional priestly duties of offering the Liturgy in some nearby parish. My dedication to theology had replaced my active priesthood for the last seven years. Nevertheless, officially retiring from the active priesthood was still emotionally rather painful. The priesthood was a real part of my identity. Giving up my priestly identity at age sixty-five left me feeling empty, useless and depressed. It was a deep loss. I felt keenly that I was not keeping my life's commitment. I was taking back my solemn word to the Church I loved. It was a feeling that followed me for a long time into retirement. For a while I could not really leave it behind.

But what I missed most after retirement was teaching. Suddenly I felt totally useless. I went into a deep depression. The break-up with Mary also contributed to my depression. With the end of my relationship with Mary I had no one to share my feeling of uselessness. In spite of my depression, or because of it, I felt a persistent need to move to McAllen, Texas. That's where I had some contacts. Besides, I might find a part time job through my earlier contacts with Sanborn Travel.

I bought an RV and a pickup and moved into an RV park in Pittsburgh. I was not there long when I decided to make my move to McAllen, Texas. On the way, I got word from my brother that my mother had died. I parked my RV and pickup and flew back to Michigan for my mother's funeral. It was a painful trip since I could not help but wonder what would my mother think about me leaving the priesthood. The funeral, with the burial at St. Mary's cemetery, was extremely sad. It took weeks for me to recover. But I returned to McAllen to live in my RV. My lonely RV trip to Texas was without incident. I had an RV directory and so had no problem finding an RV park on my way to McAllen. Traveling with an RV was a new adventure. But I adjusted quickly. My RV had a TV and I did not mind doing my own cooking. After all, I had been doing that for twenty years.

I arrived in McAllen, TX, in late June, 1993. I found a RV park and almost immediately started looking for a job. I went to Sanborn's Travel and was soon hired as a Tour Director. This meant that I was in charge of some of the Sanborn Tours going into Mexico. I was assigned an office in Harlingen to sell and sign up the tours leaving from that part of Texas. I had to coordinate my sales with the main office in McAllen. But that meant a simple phone call.

I had to do some research on the various cities in Mexico that we would pass on our itinerary. But I enjoyed that part of the job since I had come to enjoy the Mexican culture during my studies in Spanish. At that time many people from the Northern part of the country came to Southern Texas to escape the snow and cold of the Northern winters. So it was rather easy to fill a bus with tourists.

It was at this time that I met my present wife, Elida. She was the mother of Charles Nelson's wife. In a sense, Charles was my boss while I worked at Sanborn Travel. So he introduced me to Elida while she was visiting her daughter. One day we had to make a car trip to Mexico and Elida came along as far as Puebla, Mexico. She was in the back seat and I was doing all the driving. But when we arrived in Puebla she suggested we write letters so that I could keep up on my Spanish. So for eight years we wrote letters, perhaps monthly. She was more faithful to the letter writing than I..

But over the years our relationship grew. I was wrestling with the possibility of obtaining laicization papers from Rome. But after reviewing the long process involved, I rejected that procedure. Besides, I had hope that, after all the changes introduced by Vatican II, Rome might relax or eliminate the celibacy law. Of course, I continued to practice my Catholic faith as I continue to do. The hoped for change in the celibacy law has vanished with the election of Pope Benedict XVI. The fact that married Anglican priests can now enter the Church does not seem to have any effect on the law itself for Roman Catholic priests.

I knew in my heart that my love for Elida was not of the same intensity as my earlier love for Mary. But my reason decided that there are degrees of love. While my love for Elida was of a lesser degree, it was, nevertheless, real love. I was aware that my love was mixed with some pity for the poor Latinos, symbolized by my Guatemalan Elida. But I was no longer looking for the perfect love. Besides, I was older now and the love experience was bound to be less emotional. So my relationship with Elida continued. Eventually, I decided my love was sufficient for a permanent commitment in marriage. Besides, psychologists tell us, we are capable of almost infinite adjustments in our relationships with fellow humans. So, I would have to be ready for an adjustment to an older woman who, like myself, was set in her ways. But my reason told me it would not be an easy adjustment.

My marriage to Elida took place in McAllen, TX, on August 28, 1993. After the ceremonial dinner at a nearby restaurant, we drove to South Padre Island for our honeymoon. We lived in my RV in an RV park while I worked for Sanborn's Travel. But both of us disliked the heat and humidity of McAllen. So in the spring of 1994 we decided to move to Las Cruces, NM. I had visited Las Cruces on an earlier trip to San Diego and I liked the climate very much.

Living in a modern RV is not difficult. I enjoyed the simplicity. We had shelter and everything we needed for cooking and bathing. The narrow simplicity never bothered my Guatemalan wife. She especially liked our mobility. We made a RV trip to San Francisco, CA, to visit her son and family. Again, it was simple. We did not have to bother her son to make up a guest room. We simply walked over to our RV parked next to his driveway. After ten days or so we headed back to Las Cruces, NM.

Driving an RV with a pickup was a challenge when we encountered heavy crosswinds. But I soon adjusted to the fact that heavy winds would sometimes jerk our pickup to and fro. But we both adjusted to the mild turbulence. Slowing down helped considerably. Night winds in the RV parks required a more difficult adjustment. But then I got used to jacking up the four corners of our RV until it was stable, with or without the winds.

After living in the RV for a year we decided to build a house in Las Cruces, NM. We have been quite content living in our new house for 16 years. Of course, we had to learn to live with some of our building mistakes. The Diocese of Las Cruces, off and on, has invited me to teach theology in its Deacon Training Program. Besides that, the Diocese of El Paso has invited me to teach in their adult formation program. I have also found time to write a book, *Healing and Developing our Multiculturalism*. Besides that, I wrote a good portion of the book, *Understanding Today's Catholic Parish,* published by Twenty-third Publications. Both books are selling well. In addition to my writing I have served as Theological Consultant to the Diocese of Las Cruces.

I also got a brief job driving the Las Cruces shuttle between Silver City and Las Cruces. This meant I had to get up at 3:30 a.m. to get to Silver City, 100 miles away. I had to pick up the passengers who were waiting for their ride to Las Cruces and then on to the El Paso Airport.

Driving a shuttle, especially when it is empty, can be a boring job. But I needed some extra income besides my retirement income to cover our medical and our household expenses. This job helped us make ends meet. Fortunately, with my bus driving experience in Spokane, WA, I qualified rather easily for driving a shuttle.

The Aging Process

I had lived a rather active life beginning as a youth on the farm. Through the seminary and on into the priesthood I had enjoyed golfing, skiing, canoeing, tennis and other activities. I had been physically active. God had blessed me with good health. It was not until after marriage that I broke my knee coming down from the roof of our house. So this meant a trip to a orthopedic specialist in Albuquerque. The broken knee was the beginning of dependency on others to help me do what I had been routinely doing myself.

Psychologically, it is quite an adjustment to feel your good health gradually fade away and then accept dependency as a way of life. But the aches and pains of daily living just grow more acute with the years of aging. The first irrational reaction is denial. "This can't be happening to me." But it's a denial that does not last. Soon I had to give up my dream of going back to flying. I was certain that with my high blood pressure, I could not pass the medical exam. Besides that, a pension and Social Security income did not allow the expense of flying. I also had to give up golfing and tennis since my right leg with total knee replacement never really healed. Soon my doctor ordered me to use a walker permanently. My legs were not reliable anymore.

Besides, the poor right knee, I came down with a severely degenerated spine. Rather severe pain ran down my legs. I finally agreed to surgery on my spine. But it was the most useless surgery of my life. Called a laminectomy, it means the removal of bone and soft tissue that were putting pressure on my spinal nerves. After surgery there was no relief from the pain.

The next most useless surgery came about two years later when the doctor operated on my enlarged prostate to stop my need for frequent urination, especially at night. The surgery was very painful but did nothing to stop my frequent urination. The only effect this surgery had was to cause impotency. I have since learned that this is a fairly common effect with this kind of surgery, called TURP. I have also heard from others my age that the prostate can grow back "after five years."

Giving up most of the dreams for retirement was painful indeed. Golf and flying were the hardest to give up. The dream of the Golden Years vanished quickly. I just had to substitute something else. So, I began to write more and more, since I could still use the computer. I decided I just have to replace what I had to give up with something I could still do at my age. That is a difficult adjustment but I feel it is the key to a happy retirement. I soon decided I did not have to give up part-time teaching. I also accepted an invitation to write a regular column for the diocesan newspaper, *Agua Viva*.

Some one asked Freud what a normal person should be able to do well. Freud answered quite simply: "*Lieben und arbeiten.*[7] ("To love and to work.") This principle, it seems to me, applies even in old age, even though one has to accept some limitations. We are created to be creative. We have our talents even in old age. It's mostly a question of discovering what they

---

7 Erik Erikson, *Identity: Youth and Crisis,* (New York: Norton & Co. 1994), 136.

are and applying them. To lean on Erikson again: It means: "an acceptance of the fact that one's life is one's own responsibility."[8]

In the midst of all the aches and pains I decided exercise becomes more important as the years go on. John Hopkins' *Health and Medical Advisor* has some helpful advise on exercise:

> An inactive life style accelerates nearly every unwanted aspect of aging. Exercise increases oxygen flow to the brain, which can elevate mood and potentially stave off depression and age-related memory loss...Strength training with machines, free weights, or resistance bands helps maintain muscle mass and bone density. Having stronger muscles also helps take pressure off weight-bearing joints.[9]

Naturally, being the only driver in our house, much of my time is devoted to running errands. Doing household duties is a continuing adjustment, since for many years I kept all that to a minimum. But I don't let my errands interfere with my exercise. I go to the an exercise gym and ride the stationary bike for thirty minutes. If I can't do that, I do the water exercises. These are less painful but rather effective. I am not an oldster who sits in the lazy-boy all day.

I think it was in the early 70's that I read Erik Erikson's *Identity: Youth and Crisis.*[10] His portrayal of life as a journey through six cycles made a lot of sense to me. The key principle for successfully passing from one cycle to the next was the need to give up some of the habits of the cycle that went

---

8 Erikson, 139.

9 *The Health and Medical Advisor*, (John Hopkins Medical Advisor, 2011), October Notes

10 Erik Erikson, *Identity: Youth and Crisis*. (New York: W.W. Norton & Company), 1994.

before. Each cycle has its unique challenges, capacities and attractions. But if we cling to them we cannot really pass into the next cycle. Thus one can appear to be a mature adult physically and remain a youth psychologically. I have no doubt that at eighty-two years of age I am in the last cycle of my life physically. But I am still in process of mentally giving up my capacities of earlier life cycles. For me happiness in old age consists in being comfortable in my proper life cycle with its strengths and weaknesses.

Surgery for Lung Cancer?

On November 30, 2010, I was advised that I had a large mass in my right lung "with malignant characteristics." So, my doctor, a pulmonary specialist himself, recommended another pulmonary specialist to do surgery. All the preparations required were a surprise. I had to do a stress test, heart test and a breathing test. But, fortunately I passed them all. No doubt my exercise routine helped me pass these tests. The doctor predicted five to ten days in the hospital. But first I had to report for the pre-op exam. That was scheduled for November 22, 2010. I passed the pre-op exam, but the next day I learned that my heart doctor did not give clearance for the surgery. Maybe the doctor is on vacation. Maybe my arrhythmia keeps him from giving his approval.

But, fortunately, my heart doctor eventually gave his clearance. But it meant the surgery was delayed one week, to January 5, 2011. I had to arrive at the hospital at 6:00 a.m. From the moment of admission the procedures seemed quite routine. The hospital is a different world. But I had been in this world before, so I was almost relieved when the nurses pushed my cart into the bright operating room. I knew the anesthetic would soon send me off to yet another world. But I was hoping and praying the doctor would be able to remove all the cancer.

I woke up in intensive care and to my great relief learned that the large mass on my right lung was not cancer, but a mass of fungus. It still meant a full week in intensive care. But I was at peace with myself, knowing that recovery was a matter of time and patience. I was discharged exactly one week after surgery. But the pain went home with me. I had a 18 inch incision on my right side. I also discovered the doctor removed one of my ribs to extract the mass of fungus. Fortunately, we now have a good supply of drugs to ease the pain. In spite of numerous side effects, the drugs go a long way to reduce the pain.

The doctor tells me recovery will take six to eight weeks, adding that for oldsters like me recovery is always a longer process. This news was a bit of a jolt to me, but I decided I could still use the computer during this recovery period.

One day returning from shopping at Walmart, I could not help but recall the many people who offered to help me reach for that box of Corn Flakes on the top shelf. They realized my need for help as I scooted around in my electric cart. Young men and young women routinely ask: "Can I get something for you?" This offer of help restores my faith in the basic goodness of human nature. A small act of kindness stays with me for the rest of the day. I have finally adjusted my attitude and internally accepted the fact that I need help. Needing help is part of the aging process. My job is to be grateful for the help and never forget to say so.

Only God knows what the coming years will bring. But I have accepted the reality that every new day brings new opportunities to do something for the Lord. I have felt the Lord's call "to go into my vineyard." I will be happy to continue my labor there, knowing that my vocation does not end until the pall-bearers come to carry my body to the cemetery. All of life, including retirement, is a daily, joyful response to "Here I am Lord, send me."

Chapter 5

The Ruminations of an Aging Professor

Except for those long hours on the farm with the tractor and plow, my life has rarely been boring. I have skied down Mt. Aspen on a fresh blanket of snow. I have been transfixed as I gazed on the Taj Mahal in India. I have enjoyed a beer at the top of the Eifel Tower in Paris. I have flown my Cessna 172 around Mt. St. Helens, WA, and gazed at the hole in its peak after it exploded. I have hunted deer in Northern Michigan; I have gazed at a beautiful deer with a wide rack of horns. Through my scope I looked at the surprise in its eyes. But with my deer rifle at the ready I just could not pull the trigger. It was such a wonderful creature! As the deer's white tail bobbed into the woods, I enjoyed a good laugh at myself. I discovered that did not have the courage to actually shoot the deer we were hunting.

I have taken the ferry from Hong Kong to mainland China to stay at the Maryknoll House. I have watched the bull fights in Mexico until I was close to tears. Never again would I pay to see such cruelty to animals. I have seen the poverty of Guatemala and the luxury of Acapulco. I graduated from College *Magna cum Laude* and later was awarded the Flannery Chair of Roman Catholic Theology by Gonzaga University. I have conducted over 300 workshops on Parish Pastoral Councils in the U.S. and Canada.

I don't know what awaits me before I say good bye to this world, but at 82 my heart is full of gratitude for the grace-filled journey I have had. I will leave this life with a happy "thank you" to God and to the many people who made my exciting journey a reality. In my mystical moments I feel my inner joy and peace is a foretaste of heavenly bliss.

My Love for the Church

I fell in love with my Church when I plunged into my dissertation for the doctorate. With my love for the Church I chose to write on Vatican II's *Dogmatic Constitution on the Church.* It was a real thrill to follow the process of the Council while it produced this fantastic document. Sometimes I felt like I was in Rome watching and hearing the sometimes heated debates.

I have always been quite aware of the human side of the Church. I knew I was ordained by an alcoholic bishop. I saw him at close range while in his drunken state. From that day on, I realized in my bones that the Church can at times seem more human than divine. But I had seen alcoholism before. So it was not much of shock to see my very human bishop in the grip of alcoholism.

I have also been aware that no matter how frail the human Church, the human will always be the apt vehicle for the divine. That is the practical meaning of the incarnation of the God-man.

For this reason, I have always been aware that I need to forgive my Church just as I forgive my scolding father. As Christians, we remember

St. Paul's wonderful phrase: "God was in Christ reconciling the world to Himself." Forgiveness is the key to reconciliation. My forgiveness is an extension of the risen Christ's continuing forgiveness.

I have never understood why Catholics change parishes just because they don't like the pastor. We just don't join a parish because we happen to like the human personality of the pastor. The presence of Christ in the parish overrides all our human reactions to Church leaders. Perhaps, it takes a deeper appreciation of the humanity of the Church in the New Testament. That St. Paul could have a fight with St. Peter reveals both the humanity and the sanctity of St. Paul.

So, after my own experience with the human Church, I do not find it hard to forgive my Church. I forgive the Church I love for the scandal of sexual abuse, for the law of celibacy and for the alcoholic priests in its sanctuaries. I forgive my Church for becoming a second Roman Empire after Constantine. I forgive my Church for the way it appoints bishops without a meaningful consultation of the gifted people of God. I forgive my Church for its retreat, under Pope John Paul II, from the grand vision of Vatican II. I forgive my American Church for not holding a Fourth Council of Baltimore as suggested by some bishops. I forgive my Church for neglecting to dialogue with other churches and with the multicultures in the U.S. I forgive the U.S. bishops for abdicating their God-given authority in allowing the emasculation of their Episcopal Conference in favor of the centralization of power in Rome. I forgive our bishops for not implementing Vatican II's *Pastoral Constitution on the Church in the Modern World.*

I forgive my Church for its tendency to focus on only one moral issue, i.e. abortions during elections. I forgive my Church for abdicating its moral authority after the encyclical on birth control in 1968. I forgive my Church for coming late to the dialogue with Islam.

I pray for forgiveness from my Church for neglecting my own prophetic vocation as a professor of theology. I pray that my Church recover and implement the wonderful vision of Vatican II. I pray for a second Pope John 23rd and for more bishops who share his vision.

I pray for the renewal of theology across the land. God's Word is divine power. It can still renew the face of the earth. The shadows grow longer now and the autumn leaves blow across the highway of life. But I know in my heart that there will be a new spring both for the Church and for the world.

Unfinished Business

Reporters, sociologists, researchers and theologians have compiled lists of topics which try to describe today's Church in crisis. Sometimes these lists overlap a little; other times they diverge considerably. No doubt an aging theologian will be allowed to compile his own list, however arbitrary. But I have no doubt that our Church, for its own survival, will have to address many of the topics in these lists some time in the near future. Since I relate so strongly to Vatican II, I have decided to call my list unfinished business in the sense that some form of Council, either national or ecumenical, will be necessary to deal with these topics. Besides that, I believe firmly with Vatican II that "Christ summons the Church, as she goes on her pilgrim way, to that continual reformation of which she always has need, insofar as she is an institution of men here on earth."[11] For a more comprehensive view of these concerns see my list of suggested readings at the end of this chapter.

[11] *Decree on Ecumenism,* Walter Abbott, Ed. *The Documents of Vatican II,* (New York: Herder and Herder1966), No. 6.

Before Vatican II our Church was in a post-tridentine mode: we were right and the Protestants were wrong. We had infallibility; they did not. With Pope Pius XII's encyclical, *The Mystical Body of Christ* (1943), we emphasized the divine nature of our Church rather than its human nature. All this produced a triumphalism which Vatican II clearly rejected during its discussions on the *Decree on Ecumenism.* This Decree calls for a change of heart and prays for forgiveness: "...in humble prayer, we beg pardon of God and of our separated brethren, just as we forgive those who trespass against us."[12] Eventually, the Council devoted a whole chapter to the Pilgrim nature of the Church. In other words, the Council teaches that we are still struggling along: "God's people are still liable to sin."[13]

The Second Vatican Council (1962-65) was probably the most significant church event in the last century. With the popular Pope John XXIII in the lead, the Council sparked wide-ranging discussions on the Church and its relation with the modern world. It also kindled a wide range of hopes and dreams across the Catholic world. It was indeed alive with the life of the Holy Spirit. It became the New Pentecost Pope John had prayed for when He opened the Council.

But the Council also left a lot of unfinished business. Of course, some of that unfinished business came in the form of unfulfilled dreams that had little theological foundation. On the one hand, some topics, like birth control, were deliberately removed from the Council's agenda. And, on the other hand, some topics treated during the Council were never implemented after the Council. All this means that many topics ended up under the broad heading of unfinished business. But, in a rapidly changing culture there will always be some unfinished

12 Ibid., No. 7.

13 Ibid., No. 3.

business. Of course, no Council can foresee what developments in the rapidly evolving world call for a conciliar response. What follows is an amateur's list of some of this unfinished business:

1. Birth Control and conscience (Inadequate)
2. A theology and psychology of sex and gender
3. The ordination of women
4. The selection of bishops
5. The exodus of Catholics from the Church
6. The law of celibacy
7. The role and authority of National Bishops Conferences
8. The role of national synods
9. The role of the laity as participants in the priesthood of the risen Christ
10. The tensions between hierarchy and democracy
11. Christian Anthropology as a foundation for a theology of human sexuality
12. The Church and the Political Order
13. Building a Multicultural Church[14]

Some of these concerns will be treated in greater detail.

---

[14] For more unfinished business see: John Allen's *The Future Church*, David Gibson's *The Co ming Catholic Church* and Miller and Stancil's *Catholicism at the Millennium.*

The Ordination of Women

By way of introduction, it's strange that theologians today are not supposed to discuss the ordination of women. In the middle ages Franciscan theologians debated all kinds of topics with the Dominican theologians. The debates were a sign of the freedom of theologians who, unlike today, were not controlled by the diocese of Rome. Theology will always serve the Church best when it's allowed the freedom, within boundaries, to debate topics that are not yet defined. Besides that, under the inspiration of the Holy Spirit we are always capable of gaining deeper insights in truths that are, in fact, defined. Theologians mine the Church's tradition to recover the wisdom of the ancients; at the same time, they are the forerunners of legitimate historical developments which are inspired by the Holy Spirit, always present in the Church.

It's healthy both for theology and for the Church for theology to support a wide spectrum of theological opinions. This will prevent theology from becoming dominated by one theological opinion, such as that of St. Augustine or even that of St. Thomas Aquinas. In the past theologians have fruitfully debated Religious Freedom, The Primacy of Conscience, Ecumenism, Theological Dissent, Celibacy, Evolution, Slavery, Usury, the Copernican Theory and Galileo. Without their debates the Church might still be supporting slavery and prohibiting charging interest on the loan of money.

Now that we are approaching 50 years since the close of Vatican II it may be time for a Third Vatican Council to deal with the unfinished business noted above plus the many new developments which have arisen due to the rapidly changing signs of the times. Preparations could well begin with each country calling a national synod, similar to the Third Council of Baltimore, to discern the needs of the faithful in their own country. Input from the people of God would add a new dimension to the agenda and to the Council's discussions. Theological developments would still play an important role. We no longer think of theology as a static body of unchangeable truths, but as a living body of truths in a dynamic dialogue and discernment with God, with the world and especially, with the People of God.

So this time theologians and bishops would be listening more to People of God before the Council convenes. This would add the fruit of the inductive method to the Council's deliberations. At the same time, it would honor the actual human experience of the People of God. While bishops would still have the final voice, they would be listening prayerfully to theologians and to the People of God. We know from the history of St. Ambrose, the bishop of Milan, that The Holy Spirit can even speak through the voice of a child. We know that the Spirit will be present, as promised, in the voice of all the baptized. When the proclaimed Word is received in faith it becomes incarnate and then we have the real Church whole and entire. The Holy Spirit will be present in a variety of ways but especially through the principle of fraternal correction. This system will keep the teaching Church on track through the storms and turbulence of secular modernity.

No doubt sex and gender in one form or another will be on the next Council's agenda. The Birth Control Encyclical in 1968 created a divided Church mostly because there was very little theological context about sex, gender and the body. There are many times in controversial matters when Catholics can follow their informed consciences. This principle is as old as moral theology. In Catholic theology there is considerable room for subjective prudential judgements.

There is a great need today for a highly developed moral theology of the body and all the psychological dynamics that revolve around gender issues. This remains unfinished business both for theologians and for bishops. Abstinence is one response to the sexual revolution. But that is quite obviously not the response of the all holy God who created gender and then said: "Increase and multiply."

Two genders from the very beginning were an important part of God's plan in creating human nature. We do not solve the sexual problem by running from the mystery of the human. The creator reveals part of the mystery of the human by creating two genders. Both genders will have to be involved in developing a truly Christian response to today's sexual revolution. Patriarchy has tried and failed. The Church needs to pick up the pieces and build a new home for the Holy Creator's human sexuality.

The ordination of women will probably be on the next council's agenda. Today's shortage of priest presiders may well be an urgent call from the Holy Spirit for the Church to move toward a new historical development. Scripture scholars have been teaching for many years that there is nothing in the New Testament about ordination either of men or of women. So the prohibition of the ordination of women is an historical development which can be un-developed when historical conditions change. History is a witness that the prohibition is simply one effect of the pathology of misogyny and patriarchy which has plagued the Church from the very beginning.

The Church has been infected with patriarchy ever since hints of chauvinism appeared in St. Paul's first letter to Timothy. Kari Borresen through her historical research has shown "that both St. Augustine and St. Thomas Aquinas advocate an androcentric anthropology centered on the man. Both regard the theory of the relationship between man and woman not from the perspective of a reciprocal relationship but from the perspective of the male. The male is seen as the exemplary sex and the nature and role of the woman are understood in terms of him."[15]

---

15 Hans Kung, *Christianity*, (Continuum International Publishing Group Inc. 2006), 433.

The human Church is always vulnerable to this world's pathologies. Neither Jesus nor the Holy Spirit has endowed our human Church with immunity from this world's diseases. The charisms of leadership given to the Church are not limited by gender. Humans do not have the power to build boundaries limiting the breath of the Spirit in the Church. The authority of the Pope cannot create truth. He can announce truth, but he cannot create it. There can hardly be any doubt that the Spirit is speaking clearly through the voice of the People of God. The Gallup Poll of 2005 tells us that 63 percent of Catholics support the ordination of women as priests; 81 percent support the ordination of women as deaconesses.[16]

"In 1974, according to the Gallup Poll, just 29 percent of American Catholics favored ordaining women, a number that jumped to 40 percent in 1979 and then to 50 percent in 1985...the rate is still trending upward."[17] No doubt with the growing shortage of priests the People of God will rally to retain the full Eucharist, the heart of our Catholic Faith.

The clear presence of deaconesses in the early Church until the year 800 could prompt further reflection. Even in Grade School we called Ordination the Sacrament (singular) of Holy Orders (Plural). Even then it was clear that the one sacrament was capable of a variety of orders. In fact, even in grade school we learned that there were four minor orders and three major orders. Thus we assumed there were seven different degrees of participation in the one sacrament of ordination. It follows from the above that deaconesses were one of the seven degrees. In fact, it is clear from this language that gender was not a factor in determining the degree of participation even in the major order of the deaconate.

---

[16] *American Catholics Today,* (New York: Rowman & Littlefield Publishers, 2007), 176.

[17] David Gibson, *The Coming Catholic Church,* (New York: Harper Collins Publishers, 2004).

Since the deaconate and the priesthood are both ontological participations in the one priesthood, the ordination of women to the priesthood is simply a movement of degree within one and the same Priesthood of Christ. Vatican II's *Dogmatic Constitution on the Church* places deacons "at a lower level" in the hierarchy, but in the hierarchy nevertheless.[18] And we know that in the Patristic Period deaconesses were very much part of the hierarchy. So the movement of deaconesses to priesthood within the one hierarchy is not exactly new from the viewpoint of theology. It is a movement of degree. This kind of movement happens every day when there is an ordination to major orders. What is new to us is discipline, not dogma.

The Law of Celibacy

The sexual abuse crisis has drawn more attention to the law of priestly celibacy imposed on the Latin Rite by the Lateran Council of 1059. That law was very much the result of powerful historical factors shaping the Church at that time: simony, lay investiture, the forgeries, patriarchy and the monastic mentality. While remnants of these factors remain, the Church after Vatican II cannot be bound by historical factors which today have become a hindrance to its mission to bring the Gospel and the Eucharist to the whole modern world.

The next council will courageously remove those obstacles which no longer build up the Church of God. Jesus tells us: "Every tree therefore that does not bear good fruit is cut down and thrown into the fire" (Mt. 3:10). Clinging to a law which in the course of history has become a stumbling block, is a hindrance to the growth of faith and the life of the

18 No. 29.

Church. Vatican II, with its revised Liturgy, has demonstrated that we have the faith to give up the old and embrace the new. In our earthly pilgrimage we are constantly called to die to the old so we will be free to respond to the Spirit's calls to the new.

On the practical, pastoral level I could make a compelling case for some celibate ministry in the Church. While the married minister is running household errands to Walmart he/she does not have the time to visit the sick in the parish. Focusing on the limited hours on the clock, I have to conclude that service to the family uses up many hours which cannot be used for service to the people of the parish. One by-product of celibacy is more freedom; but this freedom is freedom for service to the people of God. The Church would, no doubt, have more eucharistic presiders if celibacy was optional. No doubt the Church would also be less patriarchal in its pastoral ministry.

A Christian Anthropology of Two Genders

The Church has a long history of denouncing heresies which deny the goodness of material creation, including human flesh. It has been a struggle to cling to the following basic truth: "God saw all He had made and indeed it was very good" (Gen. 1:31). The Church had to fight the dualist heresies like Manichaeanism, Gnosticism and Albigensianism to defend that simple truth of Genesis. So it has not been easy for Catholics to cling to the positive goodness of holy creation, including two genders.

But that original goodness of human nature is the basis for a sound Christian anthropology which, in turn, is the basis for understanding the Christian approach to the two genders. "To be human is to be in relation.... No human being can claim to experience or understand the mystery of what it means to be human only from his or her own humanity. The real humanity of each person, male or female, is something that points beyond itself to a real other...We are whole and entire only in our relationships with others: both human others and with God, that divine other."[19] Sin has weakened human nature, but it has not destroyed the original goodness of creation.

Two genders make up the human. A single gender, male or female, is not fully human. So the Christian view of human nature always has to include both genders. Christianity needs first to witness to the whole of humanity. A moral theology which is based on only one gender is defective. To correct our theology we need to recover the correct starting point. Otherwise, our theology will be a one-sided view of humanity. This kind of theology will never adequately serve the full created humanity.

The Church's message on sex and gender needs first to reflect on the wholeness of humanity, male and female. Only then will it be able to serve as a moral guide to humans. Sexuality is a sign that we were all created to be with another human. We are not complete without this relationship. While our vision of humanity as created is incomplete, it will be impossible to guide humans to a healthy and wholesome moral life. The next Council will have to recover a Christian vision of humanity. That will not be an easy task after so many years of a one sided, i.e. male-sided, vision of the human.

This has been especially true for the theology of love and marriage. St. Augustine assigned sexuality to the animal level. He saw nothing human in the sexuality of male and female. So for centuries the Church taught that the primary purpose of marriage was the procreation and education

---

[19] John R. Sachs, *The Christian Vision of Humanity*, (Collegeville, MN. The Liturgical Press, 1991), 20.

of children. It was this purpose which justified the "animal" pleasure of sex. The Church's teaching on sex was one sided, geared to lifting it from the animal level by various methods of rationalization.

Vatican II's *Pastoral Constitution on the Church in the Modern World* presents a more wholesome view of sex, love, gender and marriage. The section on "Conjugal Love" (no.49) represents a great leap forward in the Church's teaching on love and marriage. It tells us that married love

> "is an eminently human one since it is directed from one person to another through an affection of the will. It involves the good of the whole person.. Therefore, it can enrich the expressions of body and mind with a unique dignity, ennobling these expressions as special ingredients and signs of friendship distinctive of marriage. This love the Lord has judged worthy of special gifts, healing, perfecting and exalting gifts of grace and charity"(No. 49).

No doubt the next Council will have to deal with Christian human sexuality. Without it the Church's teaching on sexual morality will continue to be ignored.

The Selection of Bishops

Since the Church is in a crisis it is more important than ever that it can rely on very competent and highly qualified leaders who have a finely tuned instinct for the changing signs of the times. So the selection of bishops is becoming more critical every day. Nowadays we need bishops who are as skilled in listening as in speaking. Centuries ago, in 256, Bishop Cyprian of Carthage tells us that the selection of bishops by the clergy and laity is a matter of "divine authority." He writes to the clergy and laity of Spain:

> "This very thing, too, we note, stems from divine authority– that a priest (actually, bishop) be chosen in the presence of the people and under the eyes of all, and that he be approved as worthy and suitable by public judgement and testimony...And the bishop should be chosen in the presence of the people, who are thoroughly familiar with the life of each one, and who have looked into the doings of each one in respect to his habitual conduct."[20]

Since Cyprian of Carthage the selection of bishops has been an extremely complicated process. Joseph F. O'Callaghan has probably done more research on this subject than any other author so far.[21] In spite of considerable turmoil, we can conclude that the priests and laity, with many exceptions, selected their own bishops at least until the papal interventions of Pope Boniface VIII (1295-1303). Sometimes, with the union of Church and State after Constantine, (313), the Emperor appointed the bishop. Many times the bishop was also a civil governor of a Roman province. The Emperor, Diocletian (304), divided these provinces into smaller districts called dioceses. Thus, the Church took over a secular district controlled by the Roman Emperor.

It's clear from history that most of the time the people of God were consulted on the selection of their bishops. Wide consultation did not always produce the most qualified bishop. Sometimes political considerations intruded in the election process. Other times, bribes and simony controlled the outcome. Only a brief review of the history of the process should teach us that the methods used for the selection of bishops should avoid secrecy and ecclesiastical politics. There should also be public criteria,

---

20 William A. Jurgens, *The Faith of the Early Fathers,* (Collegeville, MN: The Liturgical Press, 1970) 1, 234

21 Joseph F. O'Callaghan, *Electing our Bishops,* (New York: Sheed and Ward, 2007)

norms or a list of qualifications which guide the selection process. The candidate should have experience in administration including personnel management. Many times the candidate needs to be bi-lingual. There should be prayerful discernment by all the people of God regarding the necessary qualifications. These qualifications should be a matter of public record. Transparency should be the order of the day. Secrecy is a major invitation to corruption, favoritism and "having the right connections."

Naturally, all candidates should be free to decline for personal reasons. They may have their own reasons, such as failing health, which require a refusal of the office of leadership. But it should be clear from all the above that the present system needs a major revision. As the revision proceeds we could do well to recall the simple directive of Pope Celestine I (422-432): "The one who is to be head over all should be elected by all. No one should be made a bishop over the unwilling."[22]

The Church and the Political Order

Vatican II's document, *The Pastoral Constitution on the Church in the Modern World,* represents a giant step forward in outlining the relationship between the Church and the Political world. Chapter II, "The Community of Mankind," Chapter III "Man's Activity throughout the World" and Chapter IV, "The Role of the Church in the Modern World" present solid foundations for relations between the Church and the Political Order. They contain the principles which should guide the teachings of the Church, especially before and during elections.

---

22 Quoted in O'Callaghan, *Electing our Bishops.* (New York: Rowman & Littlefield Publishers, 2007), VI.

The separation of Church and State does not mean the Church abdicates its prophetic responsibilities to hold elected officials accountable to the natural law, to the principles of social justice and to the *public* common good. These principles cannot be ignored even at the risk of accusations of partisanship.

"Politics" Webster tells us "is the art or science of government." The word comes from the Greek, *polis*, the city-state, which referred to the city and to the citizens of that locality. In a democracy all citizens, including church leaders, have the right to participate in the art of governing their city-state. Dictatorships arise in the vacuum created when average citizens abdicate their responsibilities

Vatican II rejected the idea of the union of Church and State which began with the Emperor, Constantine, in 312, and continued through Vatican I (1869-70). But even though the Church has blessed the separation of Church and State, that does not mean that the Church must maintain a passive role in the affairs of its city-state. On the contrary, it is bound by its own teaching on social justice to contribute to the welfare and the public common good of its own city-state. In the modern world the monastic model for the Church will not fulfill its mission to the world. The Church cannot be in flight from the world and still fulfill its God-given mission to defend human rights and preach social justice to the real world. It would be helpful for all bishops to have pastoral experience in a Mexican *barrio*, or, at least, to take a slum tour to Africa. This would add the blood and tears of reality to their teaching on social justice.

The National Bishops Conference

The authority of the National Bishops Conference needs to be restored. While it is not a form of collegiality as defined by Vatican II, it is, nevertheless, a fraternal sharing of pastoral wisdom which is fruitful for building up the National Church. After all, Vatican II had defined the Conference of Bishops "as a kind of council." So it was a sad day in 1998 when Pope John Paul II issued his *motu proprio, Apostolos Suos*. It reduces the authority of Bishops Conferences to the point where bishops become the Pope's altar boys. From that day the power of Bishops' Conferences by papal fiat is only delegated power. Of course delegated power can be limited by law, by papal fiat or withdrawn entirely.

This decree nullifies most of the power Vatican II gives to the bishops[23]. It is one more step in the centralization of power in Rome and a retreat from the grand vision of Vatican II. This centralization of power is detrimental both to the individual dioceses and to the Universal Church. There is a great need for a Council to define what is the foundation for the Universality of the Church. In the early Church it was based on one Lord, one Eucharist, one Gospel, one creed and one brotherhood in the Lord. The Church proclaimed its universality through the four marks of one, holy, catholic and apostolic. The whole church clings to the apostolic teaching, to the Word and to the breaking of the bread. Before Vatican II many people thought that Latin in the Liturgy was a sign of its universality. But all that changed with the introduction of the vernacular Liturgy.

The centralization of power in Rome cannot be a sign of universality since, for many centuries, the Diocese of Rome was no different than other dioceses across the Catholic world. Universality is best understood,

---

23 For more details see Ladislas Orsy, *Receiving the Council*, (Collegeville, MN: The Liturgical Press, 2009.), 16-18.

not geographically, but in a unity of love and faith in the same teaching across all borders.

Ultimately, universality must be based on faith in the one risen Christ. For this reason, the National Conference of Bishops must recover the jurisdiction they receive as individual shepherds and pastors of their own dioceses. They cannot lose their power because they gather in unity to discuss pastoral problems. Praying one and the same creed, celebrating the one Eucharist and believing in the one risen Christ, they are a sign and symbol of the universality of the Church.

This symbol does not need to be a numerical or geographical representation of the whole Church to be a valid symbol of the universality of the one Catholic church. While some centralization will always build up the Universal Church, this centralization does not require legalistic control. It would be healthier for the Universal Church to support indigenous churches as they arise in the different cultures around the globe. The N.T. Church did not impose the Law of Moses on the Gentiles. Unity with Jews and Gentiles was achieved through common faith and the breaking of the bread. St. Paul is our best witness to the universality and Catholicity of the Church.

The Exodus

With today's widespread custom of Bishops closing or merging parishes, it should be no surprise that the Catholic Church is experiencing a serious exodus. The fact of the exodus is fairly well established by sociologists' research. Some of this research is published in *The Search for Common Ground.* Other surveys are contained in *American Catholics Today.* This last book, in a long appendix, provides the raw data from a 2005 Gallup

Survey. David Gibson in his book, *The Coming Catholic Church* goes a little further and asks: "Why they are leaving."[24]

First, Gibson provides some statistics to prove the actual exodus. But then he explores the many diverse reasons why Catholic leave. He has a category, called "defecting in place" which I find quite helpful in understanding what is actually taking place, namely, that many Catholics still call themselves Catholic but no longer accept the Church's moral authority. They believe, for instance, that you can be a Catholic without accepting the Church's teaching on abortion. Gibson explains "defecting in place:"

> The same trend toward detachment was reflected in a question on who has the final moral authority, church leaders or the individual. Across the board, on issues ranging from homosexuality to sex outside of marriage to remarrying without an annulment, Catholics have steadily shifted away from giving that power to a cleric and are instead claiming it for themselves.[25]

All this presents a challenging question: What do we do about it? First, it seems to me, we need to explore in greater depth, why Catholics are leaving. Statistics reveal that Latinos are leaving the Church at an alarming rate. Gibson gives us some of their reasons: "...Latinos often find themselves with no voice in the institutional structure, and isolated within the dominant white European Catholic community."[26]

---

[24] David Gibson, *The Coming Catholic Church*, (New York; Harper Collins Pub. 2004).

[25] Ibid., 66.

[26] Ibid., 75.

There is no doubt that American individualism has infected American Catholicism. *The Search for Common Ground* quotes a typical woman from Indiana: "It's not necessary to follow the Church's teaching regarding sexuality. It's up to the individuals involved as long as no one gets hurt. It depends on the circumstances."

But we still need to answer the question: What to do about the exodus? It seems to me there needs to be a new evangelization program launched by each diocese. This program would require special instructions to a team of adults who would go from door to door throughout each diocese. They would be given a list of the typical questions they would probably have to answer at the door. But that would deal only with the intellectual side of the problem.

They would also need to volunteer to take the questioner to church with them next Sunday. They would also promise to pray for them while they invite them to return. Each parish could have a special celebration for those who return to the community of faith. The celebration could begin with the proclamation of the return of the Prodigal Son (Luke 15:11-32) which ends with a celebration.

Multiculturalism

One cannot go to Walmart these days without experiencing the multiculturalism of our democracy. This dimension of our American culture is bound to grow in the years ahead. We need to honor the garden salad model rather than the melting pot. Our unity is not conformity in externals such as language or customs. Our bonds of unity transcend externals. We may cling to our forms of personal and communal prayer, knowing all the while that another culture may worship the same God in their own way. We need to honor the different cultures by honoring their art, their language and their cultural symbols. We cannot impose our Western symbols on Africa or China as if that were a requirement for belonging to the true Church.

At the same time, we need to be careful that we do not adopt a particular culture with its symbols and legal system without some critical discernment. The Church knows full well that all cultures have their share of weeds that must be sifted from the wheat. If the Church becomes inculturated in one culture, that same culture may become an obstacle to honoring other cultures. So it must achieve inculturation with a holy detachment, knowing that the Church cannot bind itself or its mission to any one culture. St. Paul brought both Jews and Gentiles together at the table of the Lord. His example continues to be a light for all of us. It has been said many times: "Unity is not uniformity." I have discussed multiculturalism at some length in my recent book, *Healing and Developing our Multiculturalism.* (Wipf and Stock Publishers.) It is an effort to apply the wonderful teaching contained in Vatican II's *Pastoral Constitution on the Church in the Modern World.*

The Role of the Laity as Participants in the Priesthood of Jesus Christ

Until the U.S. Bishops published their fine booklet on *Lay Ecclesial Ministry* in 1999 very little had been done to implement Vatican II's wonderful theology of the lay priesthood. This teaching was part of Vatican II's *Dogmatic Constitution on the Church.* But so far very little of the theology in the U.S. Bishop's booklet has taken concrete organizational form at the parish and diocesan levels. However, there have been a number of spontaneous lay organizations which continue to grow. Besides that, some dioceses have lay ministry formation programs which award a certificate in theology. or Pastoral Ministry. So the graduates are ready to teach catechists and to make up for the priest shortage by accepting other ministerial assignments in their parishes.

Lay Ecclesial Ministry contains some wonderful theology. For instance, it tells us:

> "Lay ecclesial ministry is experienced by many to be a call to ministry, a vocation. It is the role and responsibility of the entire Church (including the bishop and the local parish community) to foster, nurture, encourage and help discern all vocations to ministry...Lay ecclesial ministry is a gift of the Spirit to the Church. The experience of the past thirty-five years can be seen as the grace-filled work of the Spirit...In general, lay ecclesial ministers should be designated by the diocesan bishop (or representative) to their ministerial assignments within the diocese."[27]

The same document recommends: "Dialogue among bishops, theologians, canonists, ordained ministers, and lay ecclesial ministers for the further articulation of the theology of lay ecclesial ministry.[28] In fact, dialogue could start by discussing the fine theology in *Lay Ecclesial*

Ministry. In many dioceses the laity's participation in the priesthood of Christ remains unfinished business. Lay specialists could be attending the annual meetings of the National Conference of Catholic Bishops, not because they are lay persons, but because they have special gifts. Bishops, in turn, could attend the annual meetings of *Call To Action* in Milwaukee,

---

[27] *Lay Ecclesial Ministry,* (Washington, The U.S. Bishops Catholic Conference, 1999) 20.

[28] Ibid., 21.

All this would surely help to heal our divided church. Bishops would recover much of their authority, lost after the Birth Control Encyclical, by careful listening to the concerns of the lay priesthood.

In view of all the above, there will have to be more adult formation classes to prepare the lay ecclesial ministers to minister with the competence and expertise the people of God deserve. A diocesan certificate would be one way to maintain the necessary quality of this ministry. The certificate means the minister has passed the required exams to qualify for his/her special ministry. Some supervisor can also attest to his/her quality of Christian life.

National Synods

On September 15, 1965 Pope Paul VI established a Synod of Bishops. This was indeed a historic step. From the viewpoint of theology it was a witness to the fruitfulness of the synodical principle throughout history. Already in the time of Cyprian of Carthage (200-258) we see the frequent use of synods, mostly to clarify the Church's teaching on baptism. The Second Vatican Council recommended the formation of National Synods in its Decree on Bishops: "This sacred Ecumenical Synod earnestly desires that the venerable institution of synods and councils flourish with new vigor" (36). The three Baltimore Councils held in 1852, 1866 and 1884 serve as a fine example of such national councils.

These national synods would include priests and laity with special expertise regarding the subjects on the agenda. The synods would require broad consultation of the people of God on the various subjects to be discussed. A Call to Action Conference was held in Detroit in 1976. Jay Dolan reports that this Conference "set important precedents and focused public attention upon the need to examine the relationship between social witness and ecclesial ministries."[29] If ecclesial ministries are going to take their proper place in the mission of the U.S. Church they will need representation at National Synods.

Catholicism at the Millennium

Considerable research has been done about the future of Catholicism.[30] But it seems that the Church, at the minimum, will have to deal with John Allen's "Ten Trends that are Revolutionizing the Catholic Church:" A) A World Church, B) Evangelical Catholicism, C) Islam, D) The New Demography, E) Expanding Lay Roles, F) The Biotech Revolution, G) Globalization, H) Ecology, I)Multipolarism, and J) Pentecostalism.[31] Besides these ten, G. Miller and Wilburn Stancil in *Catholicism at the Millennium* give us a brief survey of the pressing issues the Church has to face today. Among them, it seems to me, "Reason and Religion" will have a high priority.

It's true, as Miller and Stancil remind us, that the Church of Tradition is in transition. How should we respond? Can we slow down the pace of this transition? Hardly. Most of the forces at work are outside of our control. Can we give some direction to the transition? Perhaps.

We still have at our disposal the power of the Word of God. The power of the Holy spirit is also on our side. Saving grace is a power that works in and through the human, however frail that may be. But this grace has to

---

29 Dolan, Jay, Appleby Scott, Byrne, Patricia and Campbell, Debra, *Transforming th Parish Ministry,* (New York: Crossroad, 1989), 277.

30 For a brief overview of current research see "Suggestions for Further Reading," in John Allen's *The Future Church*, (New York; Doubleday, 2009)

31 Ibid., Table of Contents.

wait on our human effort. So we cannot sit back and expect miraculous interventions.

There is a great need, as Gerald Miller reminds us, for the Church to address "the human condition in the light of the Gospel."[32] The U.S. bishops need to update their wonderful Pastoral Letter, "Economic Justice for All," issued November 27, 1986. It is not easy to teach Catholic Social Teaching so that it takes root in the Catholic conscience. Until Vatican II the Church has been turning inward, more concerned about defending the faith in a Protestant and secular environment than reaching outward toward the changing culture around it. So devoting our energy to implementing the Church's teaching on Social Justice will require a difficult conversion for many Catholics. The Social Justice encyclicals of Pope Leo XIII and Pope Pius XI need an American revision with specific applications to our own wounded cultures.

Since I witnessed the wonderful powers unleashed by Vatican II, I am a firm believer that Catholics gathered in synod or council will be able to discern both where and how their transition should go. But history is a witness that doing nothing will not do. After we kneel and pray, we have to get up and roll up our sleeves for the task ahead. We need both the power and the will to act. I'm sure we have both.

---

32 Gerald Miller, "Catholic Social Teaching at the Millennium: The Human Condition in the light of the Gospel." *Catholicism at the Millennium*. (Kansas City, MO: Rockhurst University Press, 2001), 126-138.

A Bibliography for Further Study

Allen, John Jr. *The Future Church*. New York: Doubleday, 2009.

D'Antonio, William; Davidson, James; Hoge, Dean; Gautier, Mary. *American Catholics Today.*

Lanham, Maryland: Rowman and Littlefield Publishers, Inc. 2007.

Davidson, James; Williams, Andrea; Lamanna, Richard; Stenftenagel, Jan; Weigert, Kathleeen; Whalen, William; Wittberg, Patricia. *The Search for Common Ground.* Huntington, Ind: Our Sunday Visitor, Inc. 1997.

Gibson, David. *The Coming Catholic Church.* New York: HarperCollins Publishers, Inc. 2003.

Miller, Gerald and Stancil, Wilburn. *Catholicism at the Millennium.* Kansas

City, MO: Rockhurst University Press, 2001.

CHAPTER 6

The Dream of an Aging Professor:

The Fourth Plenary Council of Baltimore

Introduction

Martin Luther King had a dream-- a dream that electrified a nation. It was a prophetic vision, a vision of racial equality. It soon caught fire in the real world. Signs like, "No Colored allowed!" came down. Laws were passed. Voting patterns changed. And so did the jobless market. Some were inspired to campaign for president of the United Sates. Blacks were allowed to run their own TV show. They were in our very own living room every day. A dream can become a vision, a vision which moves the multitudes to new life, a rebirth in the Holy Spirit.

Maybe a man who has been in the Catholic Church for 82 years is allowed to have his own dream–this time about the Church. My dream takes the form of practical renewal through a grand assembly of the People of God. The people will come together at the ringing of the bells– young and old, men and women, fat and skinny, grandma and grandpa, bishops and altar girls, handsome and crippled.

They are the ones who sing the alleluia on Easter and cry at the pastor's funeral. They bring the salad for the church supper and they wash dishes when all have left. They call the numbers at the church bingo and turn off the lights when all the prizes are gone. They teach catechism on Saturdays and Sundays. The parish goes on, one lurch at a time. Some how Jesus would find a home here because these are the kind who sat with Him on the mountain of the beatitudes. And they will come to the mountain once again when there is a Fourth Council of Baltimore. The Lord is calling!

Bells for a Plenary Council

We noted in the last chapter that the three Plenary Councils of Baltimore were all held in the short space of thirty-two years (1852, 1866 and 1884). Of course, the American Church at that time still had a lot of business relating to its founding as a country and as a Church. Nevertheless, our own U.S. history is a witness to the usefulness of Plenary Councils. They build up the Church and generate a spiritual energy which spreads throughout the U.S. Church. We cannot forget that Vatican II recommended that "the venerable institution of synods and councils flourish with new vigor. Thus faith will be spread and discipline preserved more fittingly and effectively in the various churches..."[33] It could also reduce the growing centralization of authority in Rome and recover the true role of the bishop in the Church. After all, the Holy Spirit will be present in all his Pentecostal Power.

There is no doubt that the Third Plenary Council of Baltimore (1884) was a major force in shaping the U.S. Church. Its long-lasting

[33] Walter Abbott S.J. Ed. *The Documents of Vatican II,* (New York: Herder and Herder, 1966), *Decree on the Bishops' Pastoral Office in the Church,* No. 36.

influence can be seen in two areas: First, the authority of bishops became almost absolute. After this Council bishops exercised almost complete control over parishes. This was, at least in part, a reaction to lay trusteeism which was especially strong in German parishes. Secondly, the Council decreed that all parishes should have a Catholic School. This was a reaction to the anti-Catholicism which was evident in the public school system. In their decrees ordering the establishment of the Catholic School system "the bishops centered on four points:1) the establishment of parochial schools, 2) the pastor's obligation in this matter,3) the people's obligation to support such schools, and finally, 4) the obligation of parents to send their children to Catholic schools."[34] This Baltimore Council serves as a good example of what a Plenary Council can accomplish. But the Fourth Council of Baltimore will be a new version of an old structure. It will incorporate the new theology of The Second Vatican Council. But it will also go beyond it to respond to today's signs of the times.

The participation of priests and laity, representing the People of God, will add a totally new dimension to the Council's discussions. They will provide a linkage with the grassroots of today's believers. Thus the whole Council will be enriched by the voices and gifts from the men and women who make up the People of God. For we know from Vatican II that the Holy Spirit "distributes special graces among the faithful of every rank. By these gifts He makes them fit and ready to undertake the various tasks or offices advantageous for the renewal and upbuilding of the Church..."[35]

---

34 Jay Dolan, *The American Catholic Experience*, (New York: Doubleday & Co. Inc. 1985), 271-72..

35 *Dogmatic Constitution on the Church*, No 12.

Who Comes to this Council?

Since Vatican II put The People of God before the hierarchy in the *Dogmatic Constitution on the Church*, we need to give the People of God first place in the process of gathering any assembly of the Church of God. Thus this Council will invite lay members of Parish Pastoral Councils to come as voting members representing the people of their parishes. Laypersons, Priests and Religious members of Diocesan Pastoral Councils will also come as voting members to represent the Diocesan Church. Priest members of the Diocesan Presbyteral Councils will come as representatives of the diocesan clergy. All these representatives will participate in both the preparation and deliberations of the Council. Finally, all the bishops who possess jurisdiction and, therefore, the power of governance, will come to share their power of governance with all the baptized, who, after all, share in the priesthood of Christ.

During the preliminary discussions with the opening of the Council, a parliamentary process and organization will have to be accepted by all. During this time the Council will have to correct an error in the new code of canon law (Can. 129) which says that only those who possess Holy Orders can possess the power of governance. It states that lay persons can only *cooperate* in the exercise of this power of governance, but they cannot *possess* the power of governance. The distinction is between *possession* and *exercise*. Only those who are ordained, according to the present wording of Canon 129, can *possess* the power of jurisdiction and, therefore, the power of governance. The *Commentary on the Code* tells us: "The distinction between possessing the power of jurisdiction and merely sharing in its exercise is new and it is not at all clear what it means to cooperate in the exercise of a power that at person cannot hold."[36]

[36] *The Code of Canon Law, A Text and Commentary*, 93

A quick look into history reveals that lay persons did in fact participate in the power of governance, that is, they possessed the power of jurisdiction. Ladislas Orsy lists some of the ways laypersons in the past participated in the power of governance which included the power of jurisdiction:

> The ecumenical councils of the first millennium, called by the Byzantine emperors and empresses, were surely acts of jurisdiction by laymen and laywomen. The majority of the participants at the Council of Florence were not "in orders;" therefore, "lay votes" had a real impact on the determinations concerning the reunion of the Eastern and Western Churches. Abbesses for centuries exercised "quasi-episcopal" jurisdiction in governing "quasi-dioceses"–except in dispensing the sacraments for which ordination was necessary. Such "lay prelates" had the "power of jurisdiction" with the full and direct support of the Holy See well into the nineteenth century.[37]

History is our witness that laypersons can indeed possess the power of jurisdiction. Thus they can vote in the council. And their vote has equal weight with the vote of those in orders. This kind of vote will be in tension with the votes of Parish Pastoral Councils which, so far, are "consultative only." However, since a Plenary Council is a totally different juridical entity, the principle of "consultative only" does not apply to the Plenary Council. Lay participants will need to resist the temptation to apply the laws of the parish council to the Plenary Council which is a unique assembly, differing mightily in it's process and constitution.

---

37 *Receiving the Council*, (Collegeville, MN: Liturgical Press, 2009), 39.

A Tentative Agenda

The final agenda for this council will come from the preparatory parish assemblies held throughout the U.S. These agendas will be submitted to the National Agenda Committee which will be authorized to screen and eliminate overlapping and repetitious items. In this way the voice of the People of God will be first on the agenda. True pastoral theology comes into existence both from below and from above. It comes from above when the Gospel, the Word of God (from above), is proclaimed in the midst of God's people. That Word becomes incarnate when the people believe and live that Word. This incarnate Word shapes pastoral theology from below. Presbyteral Councils and Diocesan Pastoral Councils will also submit their agendas to the National Agenda Committee. What follows are suggestions from one aging theologian for such an agenda. They do not have any priority, but come as a continuation of the ruminations of the previous chapter.

Indigenous Churches

If we take our multiculturalism seriously we need to build a Catholic Church which nourishes indigenous churches. The theology of these churches has been well explained in Appendix II by Dr. Maria Aquino in my book, *Healing and Developing our Multiculturalism*. No doubt, the first of such churches would be for the growing Latino population. There is no reason why the Church could not establish a personal prelature similar to the Military Ordinariate which would have jurisdiction over these churches.

This Latino Prelature would honor not only the language of the Latinos but especially their unique culture. These indigenous churches would be fertile ground for indigenous leadership, including bishops, priests and lay ecclesial ministers. Dr. Aquino notes that there are "more than fifty million indigenous people across the Americas who speak 500 different languages. They are neither the remnant of an extinguished people nor insignificant minorities. They have not been annihilated but represent the most consistent human population in the midst of an evolving society."[38]

The era of the melting pot is over. While the Church can support assimilation, this does not mean indigenous peoples need to abandon their unique cultures. A healthy democracy can encourage the preservation of unique cultures within its boundaries. Each culture enriches our democracy. Diversity would follow the model of the garden salad, rather than the melting pot. Healthy assimilation can accommodate a diversity of cultures. But indigenous churches could lead the way. The Fourth Plenary Council of Baltimore could deal with all the structural and ecclesial issues involved.

The Role of Women in the Church and Society

Unfortunately, the Church so far has not done much to lead the way in instituting official leadership roles for women. Male clergy still dominate. I have worked with women theologians over the years at two universities. No one can deny their competence for leadership roles in the Church. Unfortunately, leadership to be accepted, still needs to be linked with ordination. However, the Church could institute different kinds of ordination which would include women. Since these kinds of ordination would be a departure from customs of the Catholic Church, it would require careful, in-depth study by our very own experts. The Fourth Plenary Council of Baltimore would require long preparation to present

---

38 Maria Pilar Aquino, *Theology and the Indigenous Cultures of the Americas: Conditions for Dialogue.* Published in *Healing and Developing our Multiculturalism,* (Eugene, OR: Wipf and Stock, 2009), 156-157.

convincing proposals for discussion at the Council. There is no doubt that deaconesses could be ordained tomorrow. The Church, especially in the East, has a long tradition of deaconesses. Preparation for this kind of ordination could be formation classes held at the diocesan level. But, since ordination is an ongoing historical development, the Church could develop other kinds of ordinations.

Thus there could be ordinations to the ministry to the sick, ordinations to catechists, ordination to the office of lector, ordination to youth ministry. All these ordinations would be based on competence, not sex. Since the present sacrament, as noted above, is an historical development, there is no reason there could not be more historical developments. The Church's ministries will remain as diverse as they were in the New Testament period. Ordination is one way of structuring the Church's many ministries and holding them accountable to the People of God.

We need to mention in passing that there is nothing in the New Testament about ordination, either for men or for women.[39] Scripture scholars agree that ordination is a post-New Testament development. So it is clear that the historical Jesus did not institute the sacrament of ordination. Ordination could continue its historical development as the Holy Spirit prompts it. In a related matter, Francis Sullivan explains: "One looks in vain to the New Testament for a basis for the idea of an unbroken line of episcopal ordination from Christ through the apostles down through the centuries to the bishops of today."[40]

A thorough study of the historical development of the sacrament of ordination might quickly reveal that the prohibition of the ordination of

---

39 Eduard Schweizer, *Church Order in the New Testament*,(London: SCM Press, 1961), 206-207.

40 Francis Sullivan, *From Apostles to Bishops*. (New York: The Newman Press, 2001), 80.

women is one effect of the patriarchy which infects the clerical culture as a continuing pathology. We know that with the help of the Holy Spirit, a new historical development can free the Church from this pathology. Then we will have a new Pentecost of the variety of gifts given to the women in our Church. Since our Church is a living body, we are prepared for those historical developments which build up the body of Christ that is the Church.

There are many leadership roles in the Church which do not require ordination to the priesthood. Women have published scholarly works which are used by professors in universities around the world. Many women have years of pastoral experience working at the grassroots of our parishes. Many are ready for more responsible leadership roles. The Council could require that all candidates possess a theological certificate or degree in Ecclesial Pastoral Ministry to qualify for a leadership office in the Church. The People of God deserve skill and competence in their leaders, male of female.

War and Peace

For centuries the Catholic Church has relied on St. Augustine's theology about a just war to justify wars started by various nations. But the Church has done little to teach the political world how to end a war. Yet, granted the tendency to start wars, a prophetic document teaching us how to end a war becomes more important every day. The Fourth Council of Baltimore could draw up a Charter for Peace. The United Nations, relying on this Charter, could be authorized to arbitrate international disputes. Civilized nations could learn that there are other ways to resolve disputes besides killing each other.

Most everybody knows about St. Augustine's just war principles, but few know about his excellent teaching on peace and peace-making. James O'Donnell in his new biography of St. Augustine gives us a rather long quotation describing part of Augustine's teaching on peace:

> For every man, even when he makes war, longs for peace, but nobody makes peace in order to achieve war. People who seek to upset the peace they dwell in do so not because they hate peace but because they want it changed to suit them. It's not that they don't want peace, but they want the kind that suits them.
>
> So peace for the body is the orderly accommodation of the parts to one another. Peace for the irrational spirit is the orderly quieting of the appetites. The peace for the rational soul is orderly agreement between knowing and doing. Peace of body and soul is the orderly life and health of the person. Peace of mortal man and god is orderly obedience under eternal law through faith. Peace among men is an orderly harmony of hearts. Peace in a household is the orderly harmony of those who dwell together in commanding and obeying. Peace of a city is the orderly harmony of its citizens in commanding and obeying. Peace of the city of the skies is the most completely orderly and harmonious coming together in the enjoyment of the presence of god and of one another in god. Peace for all things is the calm that comes from order.[41]

The Council could lead the way to St. Augustine's peace. The Charter for Peace could be required reading in every Catholic school and university

---

41 James J. O'Donnell, *Augustine.* (New York: Harper Perennial, 2005), 259.

throughout the country. History will judge us harshly if we are silent while our country is spending our tax money on wars without end. NETWORK, a Catholic lobbying group, has been established in Washington for many years. This NETWORK could serve as a model in promoting the Charter for Peace throughout the land. We are a civilized and predominantly Christian society. We need to speak out forcefully to avoid returning to a jungle existence of constant killing.

Ecology

It hardly needs saying today that we must bend all our energies to save our spinning planet which God has created. God's words at creation are still commands to all of us on this earth: "The Lord God then took the man and settled him in the garden of Eden, *to cultivate and care for it."*

(Gen. 2:15). The words, "to cultivate and to care" have a broad meaning here. Denis Edwards explains:

> The language of cultivating and caring for creation can include the many ways in which human creativity is used for the good of the community of life on Earth. It includes not only farming with best land-care practice, but also cooking, gardening, building, painting, doing science, teaching, planning, taking political action and many other creative actions."[42]

There is a real sense in which we need to learn to be creative regarding our part in God's continuing creation. "Caring and cultivating" are forms

[42] Denis Edwards, *Ecology at the Heart of Faith* (Maryknoll, NY: Orbis Books, 2006), 25,26.

of being creative about how we preserve God's original, holy creation. "Jesus teaches that God feeds and clothes each bird of the air and each lily of the field (Matt. 6:28; Luke 12:27) and speaks of God's care for every individual sparrow that falls to the ground. (Matt. 10:29; Luke 12:6)."[43] The Fourth Plenary Council of Baltimore could issue a document, similar to the Vatican II documents, dealing with both the theology and the practice of preserving our fragile earth. Time is definitely not on our side. After reading Genesis, it's clear the Church does not need any further mandates from the Lord.

The Search for Inter-faith Unity

It's been over thirty-five years since a Muslim student from Iran at Gonzaga University helped me move my earthly possessions into an apartment closer to the university. When we finished the job, I invited him and his friend to a pizzeria for pizza and beer. We had a very enjoyable dialogue about the Muslim faith. But my Muslim friend also had many questions about our Catholic Faith. So our pizza conversation turned into a real inter-faith dialogue. I was simply amazed to hear how much we had in common with the Islamic Faith.

Vatican II published two documents which are quite pertinent in the search for inter-faith unity: 1) *The Declaration on the Relationship of the Church to Non-Christian Religions;* 2) The *Decree on Ecumenism*. The first includes: Hinduism, Buddhism, Islam and Judaism. The second includes all the separated Churches and Communities who believe in Jesus Christ.

---

43 Ibid., 51-52.

Regarding the non-Christian religions the Declaration tells us: "The Catholic Church rejects nothing which is true and holy in these religions...they often reflect a ray of that Truth which enlightens all men."[44] Regarding ecumenism, the Decree tells us that "Catholics need to acquire a more adequate understanding of the distinctive doctrines of our separated brethren...Of great value for this purpose are meetings between the two sides especially for discussion of theological problems, where they can deal with each other on an equal footing."[45]

Regarding the foundation for the search for unity, Vatican II did most of the work. Our Fourth Council of Baltimore simply needs to build on that foundation. It needs to set up some structures which provide a continuing linkage both with non-Christian religions and with our separated brethren. This linkage may take the form of continuing dialogue and the form of working together on common concerns, such as war and peace, ecology, poverty, abortion, etc.

It would be helpful to follow Vatican II's twofold distinction between, non-Christian Religions and our separated Christian brethren. Thus our steps toward unity will include continuing dialogue and working together on common religious goals.

On the practical level we need to conduct adult education classes which include the two classes of people noted above. For example, small group discussions between Muslims and Catholics would no doubt be a great step forward in mutual understanding. Starting at a very elementary level they could use *Islam for Dummies* by Malcolm Clark as a discussion text. They could also read parts of the Koran to become more familiar

---

44 Walter Abbott S.J. Ed. *The Documents of Vatican II, The Declaration on the Relationship of the Church to Non-Christian Religions,* (New York: Herder and Herder, 1966), 662.

45 Abbott, *The Decree on Ecumenism*, 353.

with the teachings of Islam. They could even pray together the prayers of the Koran, for example:

> "Praise be to God, Lord of the worlds!
> The Compassionate, the Merciful!
> King on the Day of Reckoning!
> Thee only do we worship, and to Thee do we cry for help.
> Guide Thou us on the straight path.
> The path of those to whom thou has been gracious–with
> whom Thou are not angry, and who go not astray."[46]

It would also be helpful for small groups to discuss the five pillars or foundations of Islam and compare them to our own Catholic beliefs and practices. . The five pillars follow:

1. Testifying (This compares to our own call to bear witness to our faith)
2. Praying. The Moslems pray five times a day: morning prayer; noon prayer; mid-afternoon prayer; sunset prayer and evening prayer.
3. Helping the needy
4. Reflecting and fasting (Ramadan)
5. The Pilgrimage to Mecca

Discussing these five pillars would quickly reveal how much Catholics have in common with Islam. It would provide food for continuing dialogue.

Our Fourth Plenary Council of Baltimore could publish guides for discussion to provide practical help for dialogue in the movement to inter-faith unity. One guide would be for the non-Christian religions; the

[46] *The Koran,* A Ballantine Book, Published by Random House, 1.

other would be for our separated Christian brethren. Common prayer, dialogue and working together on common values is bound to bring the various groups closer together. Perhaps the best text in print today is Peter Phan's fine book, *Being Religious Interreligiously.* It has an excellent explanation of "Multiple Religious Belonging and a Theology of Religious Pluralism" (P.60). It would also be a fine book for more advanced group discussion.[47]

Wayne Teasdale, in his wonderful little book, presents the Church as "Architect of the Community of Religions" and the "Church as Matrix: a new Model."[48] He moves all of us into the future with "conversations across traditions." Joan Chittister, commenting on the Teasdale book, tells us: "This book is one of the most comprehensive, most readable overviews of the history, principles, and problems involved in ecumenical discussion in the Catholic tradition."[49]

There is no doubt that many Catholics need to do serious preparation for fruitful dialogue among the various faiths. Since we have assumed for so long that "we were right and they (all the others) were wrong, many of us are just not prepared for dialogue on an equal footing. For this reason it would be helpful if the Council were to publish a list of recommended reading as preparation for inter-faith dialogue.

---

47 See also Miller and Stancil's *Catholicism at the Millennium*, (Kansas City, MO: Rockhurst University Press, 2001) 191-206.

48 Wayne Teasdale. *Catholicism in Dialogue,* (New York: Sheed and Ward, 2004), 141 and 145.

49 Joan Chittister's comments on the back cover of *Catholics in Dialogue.*

Pastoral Sociology

For centuries theology has been in a deductive mode. The main principles came from above, i.e. from the top of the hierarchy. This principle became more sacred after the definition of Papal Infallibility. The textbooks used in the seminaries were designed in a post-tridentine mode i.e. to defend our unchanging truths against the Protestant reformers. Papal Infallibility was expanded to include papal encyclicals. The Church was proclaiming the static truths of revelation which came "from above." Theology as a science paid no attention to the voice of the faithful coming "from below." Sociology, therefore, had nothing to offer developing theology which had its own direct line to God.

All this had to change after Vatican II proclaimed the priesthood of the faithful in its *Dogmatic Constitution on the Church.* It went further and proclaimed:

> The body of the faithful as a whole, anointed as they are by the Holy One, cannot err in matters of belief. Thanks to a supernatural sense of the faith which characterizes the people as a whole, it manifests this unerring quality when from the bishops down to the last member of the laity, it shows agreement in matters of faith and morals.[50]

The key phrase is: "the last member of the laity." It means that the baptized laity, participating in the priesthood of Christ, have a significant voice in the formation of pastoral theology. So, pastoral theology, due to the incarnation of the Word, also grows "from below."

The enfleshment of the Word in the lay believers is, itself, revelatory.

---

50 Abbott., S.J. *The Dogmatic Constitution on the Church.* No. 12.

All this means the Church needs to honor the science of sociology in its pastoral ministries. Vatican II in its *Pastoral Constitution on the Church in the Modern World* tells us:

"In pastoral care, appropriate use must be made not only of theological principles, but also of the findings of the secular sciences, especially of psychology and sociology. Thus the faithful can be brought to live the faith in a more thorough and mature way."[51]

As preparation for the Fourth Plenary Council of Baltimore, the Church needs to do a lot of sociological research about the actual needs of the priests and faithful. The Council will need to respond to those needs, otherwise it will not be a truly pastoral Council. For instance,

> "the priest shortage has been documented and forecast for years...Pastoral sociologists study this kind of trend and other pastoral matters in order to uncover pastoral realities and plumb causes and consequences, the kind of information essential for informed response to pastoral needs."[52]

Only professional research will uncover the real needs of the people in the pew. The Council cannot respond in a truly pastoral way unless it knows the needs of today's people.

As an example, Robert Mahoney lists six "red flag" areas of pastoral sociology's concern:

1. "The need for Professional Research Assistance
2. Socialization of the Faithful

---

[51] Abbot, Walter. *The Documents of Vatican II.* (New York: Herder and Herder, 1966), 62

[52] *Catholicism at the Millennium.* Robert Mahoney, "Pastoral Sociology at the Millennium: Challenges and Opportunities." 96.

3. Evangelization, 'Sharing the Good News.'
4. The Vocation crisis
5. The Loss of Pastoral Symbols
6. Sanctity of Life."[53]

This kind of list is the barest beginning of the pastoral needs that still need to be discovered through professional research. Those who come to the Council will need to devote considerable time to studying the data supplied by this research. Their pastoral response will then be shaped by the actual data supplied to the participants before the Council starts. If the Church is in a crisis, as many authors believe, then it has to make a good diagnosis of the crisis before it offers a response.

Global Catholicism

Maybe it's the Internet. Or maybe it's the TV. But the teenager next door can communicate with his friends in China. In fact, with world travel and world commerce we may get the feeling that China is actually next door. Today many authors are looking into the future and asking what does it all mean for us today.[54] There is no doubt that we are moving toward a global Church. There is also no doubt that within this global Church the South will dominate. According to UN projections, Brazil with a population of 215 million by 2050 will be the largest Catholic nation in the world.

---

[53] Ibid., 114-116.

[54] Be sure to read John Allen Jr.'s *The Future Church*, (New York: Doubleday, 2009), 13-53.

Having spent considerable time in Mexico and Guatemala, I continue to be amazed at the growth of these Southern cultures. In spite of streaks of superstition, these cultures carry with them many deeply Christian values. Pentecostalism seems to grow faster every year. Many Catholics end up with the Pentecostals because they like the emotional, "ecstasy" element which Catholicism lacks. Whatever the future holds, Global Catholicism will have to be on the agenda of the Fourth Plenary Council of Baltimore. U.S. Catholics are aware that they are a universal and missionary Church, not a congregationalist island. For them Brazil and China are indeed next door. Offering hospitality will always be part of the Christian vocation.

The Sexual Abuse Scandal

Much has been written about the sexual abuse crisis. Not all of it has been helpful. Some authors are anxious to assign blame. But there is no doubt that the bishops have lost considerable credibility in the eyes of lay persons. For example CARA, (The Center for Applied Research in the Apostolate) took a survey in 2006 regarding lay attitudes toward the scandal. "Fully 62 percent said the bishops are covering up the facts."[55]

In a sense it's understandable that bishops would try to protect their priests. In the pastoral realities of daily life, bishops and their priests are family. So, the first instinctive reaction could well be denial and then protection both from civil and canon laws. There may even be a naive hope to protect the laity from the scandal. This hope is rather disconnected from our open U.S. culture. These days secrecy goes nowhere. Attempts at

---

55 *American Catholics Today*, D'Antonio, William; Davidson, James; Hoge, Dean; and Gautier, Mary. (New York: Sheed and Ward, 2007), 71.

secrecy in this postconciliar age are viewed as protection of bishops as well as betrayal of promised service to the People of God.

So, the Fourth Plenary Council of Baltimore will just have to address this problem. The scandal is moral, civil, cultural, religious and ecclesiastical. So it cannot be solved by ecclesiastical authority alone. All Catholic and civil authorities have to bend all their energies to search for the cause and then search for the solution.

The Council may need to call on experts in various sciences to find the real cause. Again, there has to be an accurate diagnosis of the problem before the bishops or anyone else attempt a solution. David Gibson makes a commendable effort to delve into the causes of the problem.[56] But he is a reporter and we can't expect him to dig out the ultimate causes, much less venture a solution. One hopeful sign for this Council will be the presence of a variety of experts, not just bishops. After all, this is not just "the bishops' problem." The People of God cannot expect the bishops to solve it alone. But a Council which is truly open to the truth, however embarrassing, can go a long way in dealing with this problem. Our human Church, in its pilgrim journey, has fallen into a deep pit. But the Holy Spirit, working through the Council, can rescue our Church and bring in a New Pentecost.

The Council's preparatory commission could set up a committee of behavioral professionals to do in-depth research before the Council begins. This research team would include the victims, the bishops, the priests, psychiatrists as well as the mothers of the victims.

Besides that, there could be a comparison study with an equal number of married Anglican priests. Perhaps celibacy is the culprit. Presently, that

---

56 David Gibson, *The Coming Catholic Church,* (New York: HarperCollins Publishers, 2004), 163-196.

is doubtful. At any rate, the Council's study commission needs the time, the personnel and the money to find the causes and propose solutions.

Social Justice

On November 27, 1986, the U.S. Bishops published a wonderful pastoral called *Economic Justice for all: Catholic Social Teaching and the U.S. Economy.* It was a follow-up on three papal encyclicals on Social Justice: *Rerum Novarum*, *Populorum Progressio* and *Centesimus Annus.* In spite of encyclicals and pastoral letters, the Church's social teaching is not well known throughout the Catholic world. The hunger and poverty in "this land of plenty" is a continuing scandal. The Council will lose all credibility if it does not address this scandal with concrete pastoral proposals.

Relativism

Pope Benedict XVI has often called our attention to the spread of relativism. It is often assumed that he is concerned about relativism in the traditional Catholic countries of Europe. However, it is clear to most professors that relativism is alive and well in the U.S. as well. Curtis Hancock has summarized the main tenets of rationalism under three headings:

a) Knowledge is, in the last analysis, merely a paradigm, a theoretical perspective constructed by culture, language or our own psychology, and therefore does not tell us what the world really is.

b) Empirical science and mathematics are the only genuine ways of knowing

c) Faith is altogether separate from reason, so much so that reason is irrelevant to matters of faith.[57]

The Council will have to address this "ism" because it is at the root of many other aberrations which undermine the faith. After teaching at two Catholic universities I can attest to the fact that relativism is a malignant disease that has infected our Catholic culture. Many students are convinced that empirical knowledge is the only genuine knowledge. It's no wonder that Sam Harris' book, *The End of Faith* was on the New York Times best seller list. There is a large audience in our secular society quite disposed to believe that faith has come to an end. Dealing with this aspect of secularism will be great challenge for the Council. It will not be enough to invoke religious authority to proclaim relativism as an error. The Council will have to defend our perennial philosophy with today's language within today's culture.

The Authority of Bishops

On may 2, 2011, the Pope fired Bishop William Morris who was bishop of Toowoomba. Australia. He got fired because in a pastoral letter he discussed the possibility of the ordination of women and the ordination of married men as a way of dealing with the priest shortage. This sudden firing of a bishop by the Pope demands some theological reflection on the independence and authority of bishops and their relationship to the Pope.

The question is not "Did the Pope act legally?" We know from the teaching of Vatican I that the Pope, in virtue of his office, has universal jurisdiction over the whole Church. So he has the authority to fire a

57 *Catholicism at the Millennium.* Curtis L. Hancock, *The Perennial Philosophy: A Tonic for What Ails us.* 49.

bishop even though the bishop does not have delegated authority. The real question is: Did the Pope and bishop Morris act with pastoral sensitivity on an issue which is not a defined dogma, but is openly discussed in the Church, i.e. the ordination of women. Open discussions can lead to historical developments which are signs of the health of the living, and changing body of Christ. Thus it may have been a good time for Bishop Morris to follow the example of St. Paul: "But when Cephas came to Antioch I opposed him to his face...for he ate with the Gentiles... and acted insincerely." (Gal. 2:11). Bishop Morris, like St. Paul, had good reason to oppose Pope Benedict "to his face" since the issue of ordaining women will be an open question until prohibition of women's ordination becomes a defined dogma of the Church. Until then, it will be a disciplinary matter open to healthy debate by bishops, theologians and the faithful.

It's quite plain in Vatican II's *Decree on Bishops* that bishops are bishops in their own right. They do not get their authority from the Pope. So they are not bishops by delegated authority. The Vatican II *Decree on Bishops* returned to the Patristic Period when bishops got their authority, not from the bishop of the Diocese of Rome, but from God. St. Ignatius, Bishop of Antioch (110) writes in his letter to the Ephesians : "It is clear, then, that we must look upon the bishop as the Lord Himself." And to the Magnesians he writes: "Take care to do all things in harmony with God, with the bishop presiding in the place of God..." And to the Trallians: "... submit to the bishop as you would to Jesus Christ."[58]

We know that Cyprian of Carthage (258) believed "that every bishop is responsible for his own actions, answerable to God alone."[59] In Vatican II's *Dogmatic Constitution on the Church* there are eight references to Cyprian

58 *The Faith of the Early Fathers*, William Jurgens Ed.(Collegeville, MN: Liturgical Press,1970), 20,21.

59 Ibid., 217

of Carthage. This tells us that the teaching of Cyprian of Carthage on the episcopacy was held in high esteem by the bishops of Vatican II. The bishop does **not** have delegated authority. He cannot be fired like a civil employee, or like the Pope's hired man. "Bishops have a *God-given authority* to which those entrusted to them should submit willingly."[60]

It's quite clear that the modern Church, these many years after Vatican II, still has not translated the Council's ecclesiology of the diocese into a pastoral reality. So it's no wonder that many lay people and priests are calling for a reform. Because of the extreme centralization of authority in Rome, the bishops are no better off than they were before Vatican II. At times they seem to have become the Pope's altar boys. We have to ask if over-centralization of papal authority is due to the habitual deference to the Pope by the bishops or if the Pope, in his own name, is re-defining universal papal jurisdiction in the model of Pope Gregory VII. One could rightly ask if the Pope has crossed the line in firing a bishop who rules by God-given authority.

The Church still has not recovered from the "overkill" of the Gregorian Reform which changed the pope from servant to the People of God to King over the Universal Church. The Fourth Council of Baltimore could restore the servant papacy of the patristic period.. Bishops, like St. Ignatius and St. Cyprian, would become pastors in their own right, "answerable to God alone." In spite of their independence bishops could, at times, defer to the principle of collegiality which also can be seen as a sacred brotherhood.

Since the papacy is being "reformed" in the model of Pope Gregory VII, the result is a creeping infallibility and an assumption that authority

---

60 Herbert Vorgrimler, Ed. *Commentary on the Documents of Vatican II* (New York: Herder and Herder, Vol. II, 232.

creates truth. The exclusion of women from the priesthood does not become a divine, irreformable dogma of the Church even if popes say so. Ordination is a human product of a long historical development. As such it was shaped by the culture's patriarchy which was a mighty power in the Roman culture. Historical developments do not become divine dogmas by a pronouncement of a pope unless the pope speaks infallibly. Who gets ordained and who gets excluded is the ordaining bishop's *disciplinary* and prudential decision. Disciplinary decisions do not become divine dogmas. An ordaining bishop could exclude all left handed or bald-headed men.

The inclusion of women in the sacrament of Holy Orders could well be the continuation of ordination's historical development. The Spirit breathes where and when the Spirit wills. The living body that is the Church needs to respond to this breathing of the Spirit or it will die. Both bishops and popes need to resist the temptation to turn discipline into dogma. The Fourth Council of Baltimore could well be the Spirit's time to continue the historical development of ordination.

The Shortage of Priests and Sisters.

Considerable research has been done to demonstrate the growing shortage of priests. It's getting late. Now we need to be more concerned about solutions than about the actual shortage. Many researchers report that the people in the pew are quite ready to accept married priests and women priests. It may be a case where the People of God's instinct of faith is well ahead of the hierarchy who are not in tune with sociology and the frightening statistics that have been published almost every where. No doubt the exodus described above will increase as long as the shortage of priests continues. It is a simple problem with a fairly simple solution. But it requires a deep faith and the courage to act. Surely the Fourth Council of Baltimore will respond to the Holy Spirit and bring new laborers into the Lord's vineyard.

Conclusions

The topics listed above do not pretend to be a complete listing of all subjects the Council will be called to address. Since the main agenda will come from the People of God, the topics listed so far serve as elementary thought-starters. The Council will have to decide what topics have to be addressed by the full Council and what topics can be handled in committees representing the People of God. The Council will also have to decide what topics deserve an in-depth treatment and what topics can be treated adequately through pastoral letters. At any rate, convening the Fourth Council of Baltimore is becoming more urgent every day. We pray daily with Pope John 23rd for a New Pentecost.

Chapter Seven

Ruminations On the Revision of our Worship

It's been thirty years or so since I read Pius Parsch's wonderful book on the Liturgy of the Mass.

For me it was a life-changing book. It inspired me and moved me to read more and more on the Liturgy. From that day on, I read every issue of *Orate Fratres,* (Later *Worship*) a magazine published by the Benedictines at Collegeville, MN. Before Vatican II it was quite exciting to read all the articles on the vernacular in the Liturgy. These articles appeared when many Catholics felt Latin was close to a divine law. But discussions about the possibility of a vernacular Liturgy continued.

House Cleaning

Since Vatican II we are all getting used to changes in the Liturgy. On December 10, 2010, Pope Benedict XVI announced another change in the language of the Liturgy. Actually it will be a new third edition of the

Roman Missal. A couple of weeks later I received an e-mail from a priest friend who was quite upset at the kind of English that was "being foisted" upon us in the new Liturgy. His letter followed a rather thorough review of the proposed English text by the London *Tablet*. He is not the only priest who is upset at the way the new English is being imposed upon the priests.

It hardly needs saying that the forms of our worship will always need to change as the years, indeed centuries, go on. True worship is always the worship of a specific culture. It is the people's worship, not only the priests'. In view of the our Catholic tradition, certain principles need to be observed during these reforms:

First, a little house cleaning may be necessary. Since our forms of worship are a human product, they are vulnerable to human accretions, human elements, which creep into the Liturgy and falsify or distort its message producing a false religious experience. Our worship is shaped both "from above" and "from below." From above comes the Word of God and divine revelation. From below comes a specific people's response in faith. That response may be a song, a procession or s simple "Amen" or "alleluia". It may also be a unique cultural response. It is of vital importance to preserve the purity of both the Word of God from above and the faith response from below.

Thus we cannot replace the scriptures with the poems of Francis Thompson, however edifying and inspiring they may be. The word from above has to be God's Word. That Word remains a sacred and inviolable element of our Worship. Only God's Word can demand and shape our faith response. For this reason, the Word of God as proclaimed, must be faithful to the approved scriptures. At the same time the faith response must also be true to the scriptures. The words, symbols and actions which make up this response will always be susceptible to a variety of subjective interpretations. And the Word, being in human form, may need to be updated, to preserve its original, sacred meaning, as the centuries go on. That's where our scripture scholars and translators serve the Church and its worship.

To give just one example, we celebrate the Feast of the Epiphany by proclaiming that the "astrologers from the east came to pay Him homage." (Mt. 2:1-6). I know of no scripture scholar today who teaches that these astrologers were Kings. (Nor does the revised *Catechism of the Catholic Church*). Therefore there is no justification on the feast of the Epiphany to sing: "We three kings from orient are." The Greek text uses *magoi* for the astrologers. And *magos*, in the singular, means: a sorcerer, a magician, a wizard ." The RSV translation calls the magi, wise men. There is no hint in the text that *magos* could mean a king. So if we sing: "We three kings from orient are," we are falsifying what actually happened during the historical birth of the Messiah. So in reforming the Liturgy, this hymn must be eliminated as part of the house cleaning which purifies the worship. Our worship needs to be true reflection of what we teach. And we do not teach that the magi were kings.

If we introduce a gap, or even a contradiction, between our catechetical instructions and our worship, we create considerable confusion in the minds of our worshipers. In short, we have to be extremely careful with the precious gift of God's Word.. Since we are human, perfect coherence between the Word and the human response will not be attainable. The response from below will often need some house cleaning. This includes new translations of that holy Word because the people's language is always in process of change. Unless the worship is alive with the actual words and symbols of a specific worshiping people, it will fall short of what the baptized people deserve.

For all these reasons those in charge of reforming the people's worship, must come from above (the scripture scholars and theologians) and from below (the average persons in the pew.)

In this way the new words will reflect correct doctrine and the correct response at the same time.

To achieve this goal, the translators need to be sensitive to the connotations and nuances the words acquire in the course of time. So it is not enough to find the correct word in the dictionary for the Latin words coming from Rome. The words need to connect with the emotions and experience of a specific people and a specific culture.

The Ecstacy Element

Researchers have discovered that many Latinos have left the Catholic Church and joined the Pentecostals because our Catholic worship has an "ecstasy deficit." As humans with a full range of emotions implanted in us by the creator, we bring these emotions to our worship. True worship, to be authentic, must include the total person. We remember that "David danced whirling around before Yahweh with all his might, wearing a linen loincloth around him. Thus David and all the House of Israel brought up the ark of Yahweh with acclaim and the sound of the horn." (2 Sam. 6:14).

Except for the occasional trumpet blast and full throated alleluias on Easter our worship still tends to be overly intellectual. It's more a worship of the head than of the heart. A true Christian community will always include the emotional component. Thus the music and song may, at times, cause an "out of body" or ecstasy experience. I will never forget that Easter morning when I was in Church for our Easter celebration. There were trumpets by the choir and songs by the whole congregation. I suddenly was swept up with emotion to a point where I felt I was in another world. In retrospect it seemed like a brief taste of heaven. The choir's outburst "He is Risen," reverberated through my whole being. I remembered St. Paul's outburst: "I know a man in Christ who fourteen years ago was caught up to the third heaven– whether in the body or out of the body I do not know, God knows" (2 Cor. 12:2-3). (Thus St. Paul is our witness that it's not only drugs or booze that provide an out of body experience) It was a pleasant awakening of my faith. Mere words in the book had become a preview of eternity. Some times the meaning of the written word does not take root without a trumpet blast or equivalent. Our faith is more than mere human emotion, but it is never without it.

The Word "from above" becomes incarnate in our lives through our participation in its celebration. It becomes a force in our daily lives through the power of the Resurrection. We ourselves become a living word. For this reason, our whole hearted participation in song, music, response, etc. is the key to good Worship. We don't just celebrate the written Word. We celebrate its meaning for us, for our community and for our world. But often the written word is the door to that meaning.

Language

In Advent, 2011, the New Roman Missal will become normative throughout the Catholic world. The translation from the Latin has been widely criticized. *America* Magazine, in a scholarly article by Paul Philibert, has called the new translation "stilted English." It calls attention to "the slavishly literal translation of the Latin. In an especially powerful paragraph

Philibert concludes: "The words do not make sense. They run contrary to the church's constant tradition of universal salvific will of Christ."[61]

This language may seem a little strong. But it is not. For it is our language that expresses our belief system. The wrong language can, in fact, be heretical. Our worship, above all things, has to be truthful before God and before our fellow worshipers. Faithfulness to the Latin text does not mean it is truthful in English.

We humans, located in our Western culture, are passing from a print culture to a visual culture. But we still communicate with each other and with our God through multiple signs, songs, sounds, lights, symbols and alas, through the written and spoken word. So if we are going to choose a common language for our worship, our worshiping community will need to engage in a long and difficult process of discernment. The slang of the street will not be the language of worship. And language tainted with irreverence will not do. Likewise, the language of the academy may be over the heads of most of us. And a literal translation from the Latin may indeed be "stilted" or worse.

What principles, then, will guide us in selecting the right words and sentence structures for our whole diverse communities? First, we need to know what are the words and sentence structures in daily use by most of our community. Our people will want to worship their God in familiar language. This language can hardly be imported from Rome or from the dictionary. But whatever language the community selects, it needs to be grammatically correct. It needs to communicate clearly and simply. Long, clumsy sentences will not do. Our culture communicates in short sentences which quickly come to the point. The worshiping people must feel at home in using the language of their worship. Heavy, Latin, cumbersome

---

61 Paul Philibert, "For You and Who Else?" *America.* (January 3-10-17, 2011), 14.

derivatives will not do. The vocabulary of worship must belong to the specific, worshiping people. That is what we mean by the vernacular.

The Greeks had many gods and goddesses. But they had one called Hermes whose job was to translate and interpret the messages of the gods for humans. Many times interpreting was more important than mere translating. If today we want to find the best modern language for worship we will also have to interpret. Mere translation will not do. Interpretation will require sensitivity to the community, to its culture and to the delicate nuances of its changing language, spoken and written.

When we proclaim God's Word, we have to proclaim it in some human form. The songs and the words will be the best we humans can produce. But that does not mean they are strange to the life of the worshipers. They will reflect the human experience present in the hearts and souls of most of the worshipers. We worship with our hearts and emotions as well as our minds and reason.

Modern languages are constantly in a state of flux because they are used to communicate between modern, living human beings. The language of worship must keep in tune with the nuances and connotations of these changing languages. Thus we changed "Holy Ghost" to "Holy Spirit." "Ghost," because of its Halloween connotation, was not a good word to refer to the third person of the Blessed Trinity. It did not communicate the reality of revelation.

For this reason the language of worship must always be evaluated at appropriate intervals. Thus we learn from the worshiping community. At the same time our worship is formed "from below." Our worship will contain words which dance, sing and cry because our worshiping community is alive with these emotions. Thus there will be a great difference between the funeral liturgy and the wedding liturgy. We celebrate joy and sadness, sometimes, on the same day.

Good worship needs to actively steer a path between a wild teenage party and a rigid military drill. It needs to leave room, within proper boundaries, for the rare ecstatic or mystical experience.

Music is part of our language. For centuries we gave high priority to the organ. But recently the guitar, the trumpet and the French horn have become part of our musical repertoire. These instruments, and many more, are part of the people's language. We praise our God with every note of the guitar, every note of the horn. Our worship must witness to the incarnation i.e. God in Jesus Christ embraced the full human condition in everything except sin. The human, now redeemed, is called to holiness. Our worship must celebrate that continuing call to holiness.

Naturally, the human voice remains the best way to praise our God. It is a total engagement of the human person, a living offering of the best we can do. Our voice may not be on the level of the opera, but our hearts provide the real meaning. And worship is a communion of hearts united in a song of praise to God. Meaning is always more important than external perfection which, in any event, cannot be achieved during our earthly pilgrimage.

EPILOGUE

We know "the powers of death shall not prevail against our (Church)" (Mt.16:18). So when we gather for our Sunday Eucharist, we proclaim with confidence that: "We believe in one holy, catholic and apostolic Church." We make this profession of faith in our Church even after the sexual abuse crisis and after other sins and human frailties of our Church. Besides that, "we confess to almighty God...." and plead: "Lamb of God, you who take away the sins of the world, have mercy on us."Yes, our Church is the body of Christ. But every body is vulnerable to the devil and to this world's constant temptations. Even Jesus did not escape the wiles of Satan.

But we also know that the mighty power of the Risen Christ through the Holy Spirit is mightily at work through this weak, frail, human Church. When we make our act of faith in our Church we profess our faith in both the human and the divine nature of our Church. Just as oil, wine, bread and water become the holy sacraments of divine life, so our very human Church becomes the sacrament of saving life. In spite of crises and turmoil, our human Church will continue to serve as God's instrument, God's sacrament, here on earth. When it falters, the power of the Holy Spirit will burst forth with a new Pentecost. This we believe with all our hearts.

This we celebrate every Sunday with our alleluias and the breaking of the bread.

When we focus too long on the human side of the Church we lose sight of the divine. When we focus too long on the divine side, we lose sight of the human. When we are smitten with the heavy doldrums of the human, we can always take flight on the wings of the poet's *Hymns to the Church*:

> "I have fallen on the Law of your faith as on a naked sword.
> Its sharpness went through my understanding, straight through the light of my reason.
> Never again shall I walk under the star of my eyes and on the staff of my strength...
> Where my feet refuse to take me, there will I kneel down.
>
> And where my hands fail me, there will I fold them.
> I will become dust before the rock of your teaching
> And ashes in the flame of your commandments...
> For where your inmost thirst would take you,
> The fountains of earth have ceased to flow...
> He who lets go of you has never known you...
> Because of you all idle wandering goes halt, and every pilgrimage finds in you its home."[62]

---

[62] Gertrude von Le Fort. *Hymns to the Church*. (New York: Sheed and Ward, 1944), 16-18.

The Call For Reform

Today we hear rather shrill calls for the reform of our Catholic Church.[63] We know from Vatican II's *Decree on Ecumenism* that we are all called "to undertake with vigor the task of renewal and reform."[64] So it's not surprising that we now have "A Lay Person's Guide to Renewing the Catholic Church."[65] After the fiasco of the birth control encyclical and the sexual abuse crisis, it's no wonder that the People of God are clamoring for reform. The sense of the faithful, thanks be to God, is alive and well. In view of the above, it's no surprise that the "Lay Person's Guide" devotes a whole chapter to "Governance in the Church." I suspect most of the People of God would agree with *The Guide* that "The Current Crisis is one of leadership."[66]

It's quite probable that the next reform, unlike the Gregorian Reform, will come "from below," from the people of God. Again, we know that "the Holy Spirit distributes special graces among the faithful of every rank. By these gifts He makes them fit and ready to undertake the various tasks or offices advantageous for the renewal and upbuilding of the Church."[67] Joseph Marren reminds us that it was the lay people who saved the Catholic Church from the Arian heresy in the fourth Century.[68]

---

63 Joseph P. Marren. *Talking Treason in Church.* (Bloomington, IN 47403, 2010), 81-97.

64 Abbot, Walter. Ed. *The Documents of Vatican II.* (New York: Herder and Herder, 1966),347.

65 Joseph Marren. *Subtitle.*

66 Ibid., 101.

67 Abbot, Walter. Ed. *The Dogmatic Constitution on the Church*, 30.

68 Joseph Marren, 39.

On February 3, 2011, 144 European Theologians signed a letter asking that the "year 2011 be the year of renewal." The letter "makes some specific demands: more synodal structures at all levels of the church; the participation of lay people in the choosing of priests and bishops; the inclusion of married males and females in the priesthood, the protection of individual rights and nurturing of a culture of rights within the church and tolerance toward single, divorced, unmarried and gay people."[69]

The letter goes on to say that the Church has lost credibility. It includes a call for democracy: "Those things that affect every one should be decided by everyone. Those things that can be decided locally should be decided there."[70] "Grassroots Catholic organizations like *Wir sind Kirche* (We are Church) have translated the letter and are organizing a worldwide petition to support it."[71] All this activity supports a growing feeling that this time the reform will come from below, from the people of God. If there is no reform or if it is delayed too long, the exodus, especially of the young and of women, will continue.

It was quite refreshing to this oldster to discover that so many theologians, heavily committed to doing academic theology in universities, would still keep alive their sense of faith in the pastoral dimension of theology. Their statement shows that they are not lost in some ivory tower, doing theology of the book.

We noted above that many lay persons feel the Church is in a crisis of leadership. Our crisis of leadership means that the method for selecting bishops will have to be subject to a thorough and painstaking review. The statement by the European theologians pleads for the participation of lay people in the "choosing of priests and bishops." The present system does

---

69 *National Catholic Reporter*, (February 18, 2011), 8.

70 Ibid., 8

71 Ibid., 8

not produce the most competent leaders. They do not earn their leadership position by demonstrating leadership skills within the people of God. They become "leaders" by appointment. They are products of the institution. Vatican II tells us bishops "are servants of their brethren." So if there is a crisis in leadership, it means a failure in servant leadership. True and honest reform will have to concentrate on a search for leaders who are truly servants in the model of the Good Shepherd. The present system is not working. The People of God deserve a new and better system for selecting their leaders.

The American Catholic culture has an instinct of faith that recognizes true leadership qualities. Robert Greenleaf said it long ago: "A new moral principle is emerging which holds that the only authority deserving one's allegiance is that which is freely and knowingly granted by the led to the leader in response to, and in proportion to, the clearly evident servant stature of the leader."[72] Our Church simply has to take servant leadership seriously in selecting it's leaders. Our leaders can no longer presume to rule by the weight of their appointed authority. Such authority simply has no weight in our individualistic culture.

Bishop Robinson's "three levels of government" deserve careful review. He offers a number of proposals for a "Government in which all Participate."[73]

Our Diocesan Church is not a monastery. But to select the best leaders our diocesan Church could borrow a page from the Rule of St. Benedict:

> "Whenever matters of importance have to be dealt with in the monastery, let the abbot summon the whole congregation and himself put forward the question that has arisen. Then

72 Robert Greenleaf. *Servant Leadership*.(New York: Paulist Press, 1991), 10.

73 Bishop Geoffrey Robinson, *Confronting Power and Sex in the Catholic Church*. (Collegeville, MN: Liturgical Press, 2008), 265-286.

> after hearing the advice of the brethren let him think it over by himself and do what he shall judge most advantageous. Now we have said that all should be summoned to take counsel for this reason, *that it is often to the younger that the Lord reveals what is best.*"[74] (Italics mine)

To adapt this principle, the chairperson of the Diocesan Pastoral Council, acting as abbot, could call together all the parish pastoral councils in the diocese. They could openly discuss the qualifications needed in this specific area of the Church. Then, after prayerful discernment, they could present a list of the most qualified candidates for an open discussion by the full assembly. When the assembly has reached a consensus, the list of the most qualified candidates could be presented to the assembly for a secret ballot.

A reform from below, to be successful, needs to be aware that there is "true and false reform.[75] True reform needs to observe four conditions to achieve authentic reform. These conditions, with detailed explanation, are listed in Congar's wonderful book. We have space here only to list the four conditions: "First condition: The Primacy of charity and of pastoral concerns; second condition: Remain in communion with the whole church; Third condition: Having patience with delays; Fourth Condition: Genuine Renewal through the return to the principle of tradition."[76]

A true reform will come primarily from below, from pastoral concerns. These pastoral concerns will require prayerful discernment by all the People of God. New methods for choosing bishops must remain sensitive to all four

---

74 *Documents of the Christian Church*. "The Rule of St. Benedict." (New York: Oxford University Press, 1963), 116.

75 Yves Congar. *True and False Reform in the Church*. (Collegeville, MN Liturgical Press, 2011.)

76 Ibid., 215- 307.

conditions. Our human church, as we know from history, is vulnerable to schisms. So the second condition, "communion with the whole church,"will always be of primary concern. Whatever method is adopted, will not be confined to one country, but will become a living structure of the whole church. And all methods will be subject to periodic evaluation. Since our Church is a living body, it is always ready for adaptation, change and new responses to the breathing Holy Spirit.

Bishop Geoffrey Robinson discusses the three levels of government. Then he offers a brief meditation:

> . . .beautiful ideas concerning participatory government, service of the reign of God within the hearts and minds of all people and the *sensus fidei* of the entire church will remain nothing but beautiful ideas unless they are given concrete expression in the daily life of the church."[77]

To get all the people to participate in the government of their church will require considerable adult education. Parish and diocesan pastoral councils represent an important step forward. However, they need to participate in diocesan synods and learn to hold their leaders accountable to synod decisions. Structural reforms will have to put together a permanent system in which accountability is simply part of the new structure. Servants have to be held accountable, otherwise they are no longer servants. There can be no doubt about our ultimate goals. Again, Bishop Robinson offers a helpful meditation: "Ideas concerning such matters as participatory government and subsidiarity, which the church constantly preaches to nations, must be applied to the church itself."[78]

---

77 Bishop Geoffrey Robinson, 287.

78 Ibid., 149.

Most of the very human structures of our institutional Church came into the Church through its marriage to the Roman Empire beginning in 313. They received a powerful blessing, indeed, consecration, from Pope Gregory VII in 1059 through the Gregorian Reform and again from Pope Pius IX in 1870 through Papal Infallibility which over-emphasized the divine nature of the Church. These structure are human, historical developments. As such they are quite capable of reform and adaptation.

Through the growing power of the media we live in a shrinking world. The 2011 revolutions in Egypt and Tunisia will soon show up next door. The people in the pew will show up on the streets. They will prove that they have advanced will beyond the days of "pay, pray and obey." Even though we go through a major reform of the human parts of our Church we can cling in faith to both the divine and the human elements of our Church. Through the baptized People of God the Holy Spirit is alive and well even through the pain and turbulence of a reform.

Let's end our memoir with a few lines from the Preface of the Funeral Liturgy:

> **Lord, for your faithful people life is changed, not ended.**
> **When the body of our earthly dwelling lies in death**
> **we gain an everlasting dwelling place in heaven.**
> **Amen.**

Bibliography

Abbott, Walter S.J. Ed. *The Documents of Vatican II.* New York: Herder and Herder, 1966.

Allen, John Jr. *The Future Church.* New York: Doubleday, 2009

Clark, Malcolm. *Islam for Dummies.* Hoboken, N.J.: Wiley Publishing Co. 2003.

Congar, Yves. *True and False Reform in the Church.* Collegeville, MN: Liturgical Press, 2011.

Cottingham, John. *Rationalism.* Bristol, England: Thoemmes Press, 1997

D'Antonio, Davidson. James, Hoge, Dean and Gauthier, Mary. *American Catholics Today.* New York: Sheed and Ward, 2007.

Davidson, James, Williams, Andrea, Lamanna, Richard. Stenftenagel, Jan, Weigert, Kathleen, Whalen, William and Wittberg, Patricia S.C. *The Search for Common Ground.* Huntington, IN. Our Sunday Visitor Publishing Division, 1997.

Dolan, Jay. *In Search of American Catholicism.* New York: Oxford University Press, 2002.

Edwards, Denis. *Ecology at the Heart of Faith.* Maryknoll, N.Y.:Orbis Books, 2006.

Erikson, Erik. *Identity, Youth and Crisis.* New York: W.W. Norton and Company, 1968.

Gibson, David. *The Coming Catholic Church.* New York: Harper Collins Publishers, 2003.

Miller, Gerald & Stancil Wilburn. *Catholicism at the Millennium.* Kansas City, MO: Rockhurst University Press, 2001

O'Callaghan, Joseph. *Electing our Bishops.* New York: Sheed and Ward, 2007

Robinson, Bishop Geoffrey. *Confronting Power and Sex in the Catholic Church.* Collegeville, MN: Liturgical Press, 2007.

Sachs, John. *The Christian Vision of Humanity.* Collegeville, MN: The Liturgical Press, 1991.

Steinfels. Margaret O'Brien. Ed. *American Catholics, American Culture, Tradition and Resistance.* New York: Sheed and Ward, 2004.

_____________ *American Catholics and Civic Engagement.* New York: Sheed and Ward, 2004.

Teasdale, Wayne. *Catholicism in Dialogue.* New York: Sheed and Ward, 2004.

Weakland, Rembert. *A Pilgrim in a Pilgrim Church.* Grand Rapids, MI: William b. Eerdmans Publishing Co. 2009.

Index